Gift

For where your treasure is, there will your heart be also.
— Luke 12:34

J.K. Wylie

© 2014

Published in the United States by Nurturing Faith Inc., Macon GA, www.nurturingfaith.net.

Library of Congress Cataloging-in-Publication Data is available.

978-1-938514-46-3

All rights reserved. Printed in the United States of America.

Unless otherwise marked, scripture references and quotations are from the Holy Bible, New Living Translation, copyright © 1996, 2004, 2007 by Tyndale House Foundation. Used by permission of Tyndale House Publishers, Inc., Carol Stream, Illinois 60188. All rights reserved.

Scripture quotations marked (NIV) are taken from the Holy Bible, New International Version®, NIV®. Copyright © 1973, 1978, 1984, 2011 by Biblica, Inc.™ Used by permission of Zondervan. All rights reserved worldwide. www.zondervan.com The "NIV" and "New International Version" are trademarks registered in the United States Patent and Trademark Office by Biblica, Inc.™

Scripture quotations marked (KJV) taken from Life Application Study Bible, King James Version. Copyright © by Eugene H. Peterson 1993, 1994, 1995, 1996, 2000, 2001, 2002. Used by permission of Tyndale House Publishers, Inc.

For Olivia, John Kinard, and Samuel…

This writing is for you, for all of those who belong to us, and for anyone else whose hands happen upon it. May it help you avoid the pitfalls in the dark and bring you closer to the light of what is real and true. We all outgrow the innocence of our childhoods and must face the realities of the world. My prayer for you is that it will not catch you by surprise and that you will be ready and equipped, to not only sort and process it, but to stand and move forward with strength and confidence in the knowledge of who you are and where you belong.

May your faces light the heavens forever! And, if I get there before you, I will be waiting with arms open wide to welcome you home — minus the wrinkles, of course! *I love you.*

In honor and in memory of my precious friends, Eva Dempsey & Roxanne Farah Keshawarz Cousins, one whose faith and boldness gave me the courage to write — the other whose faith and quiet strength gave me the courage to finish.

Contents

Preface vii

Chapter One
    POVERTY 1

Chapter Two
    FEARLESS 9

Chapter Three
    ONE EXPECTATION 17

Chapter Four
    FREEDOM! 29

Chapter Five
    DYING WITH GRACE..41

Chapter Six
    COURAGE OF PRESENCE 49

Interlude
    THE BRIDGE BUILDER..67

Chapter Seven
    PROVING WISDOM..69

Closing Prayer 81

Suggested Reading..83

Preface

*Dedicated to my husband, Phil, who without,
I would have no story to share.*

As I sit down to write and compile writings from over the past five years, it is early November in the year of 2012. I am 44 years old, but feel like just a girl.

I have been married for 17 years to my husband, Phil, who is eight years older. He is a wonderful man, a faithful husband and devoted father. We have three children, a daughter and son by birth and one son by adoption.

Our life together has been difficult and wonderful. Difficult because, well, marriage is difficult; we both have issues and are different in many ways. Wonderful because we share a love for God and both desire to live in a way that blesses and pleases Him. That has brought us much joy and peace though sometimes it takes a real effort to remember what we know to be true (but would rather forget for just a moment while we take things into our own hands)! We have found that when we choose to love each other, our understanding and affections follow course. How thankful I am for this. It would be impossible without the greater love we both have for Jesus, and I am certain it is the only reason we are still married today.

Phil was working for a power and light company when I met him. I knew immediately he was a man of integrity and walked confidently in his own skin. I liked that. He was very handsome, a manly man, with an unusual genuineness that shined in his eyes. The first time we met, he had been working long hours for 13 days straight after an ice storm had taken out the power in most of our area. He had on coveralls, a huge jacket, a toboggan, and large boots. I couldn't see anything except his mouth, nose, and eyes because of the hat and the scruffy beard on his face. He was a sight and he was at my front door!

I had ruined an anniversary dinner for my parents and smoked up the apartment my younger sister and I were sharing at the time. Even though it was cold, I had opened the windows to air things out. Phil was driving by on his way home from work and saw the cars in front of my apartment and the windows open. He figured I was having a party and decided to drop in. I was the new girl in a small town. He knew me and knew where I lived, but I didn't know him. He was surprised when my dad opened the door. At first glance, I thought he was lost and needed some directions, but the first words out of his mouth proved I was wrong and showed his extremely quick wit. After he made us all laugh and I saw those sparkling eyes and handsome smile, I was glad he was looking for me.

El Dorado (a small town in South Arkansas) was my hometown and I loved it as my hometown, but I had sworn never to return after high school. It just didn't hold for me the things I was looking for in life except, of course, my family. But I knew they would always be my family no matter where I lived. Visiting was fine — not residing. I had only lived in El Dorado for less than a year for what was supposed to be a short respite. I wasn't looking for a husband, at least not there!

I was looking for greener pastures: a contemporary work culture, nice restaurants, good shopping, a larger city where I could blend in and take advantage of the broader opportunities it would afford. I also planned on completing my education with a doctoral degree and had pretty much decided on the place when my life took a drastic detour. I met Phil, got married, and never left.

Phil was different. As I mentioned, he had a very clever sense of humor that I found refreshing. He was also an outdoorsman; I would say more specifically, a woodsman. He enjoyed being in the woods and hunting with a bow — two things that were unfamiliar to me. He listened to country music but also enjoyed the symphony, and preferred a truck though he drove an SUV when we met. Though he wasn't interested in going to parties, he would go with me on occasion. He didn't drink as a habit unless it was water or orange juice and was disciplined, open-minded, and content.

It wasn't until we had been married for about a year that I noticed Phil never wrote anything down, and when he did, it took some effort to read it. He didn't read much, and sometimes missed information that was spoken to him or omitted information that he was trying to express. On top of it, he lost his temper quickly when there was a breakdown in communication and would give up rather than talk it through.

It finally hit me (a speech-language pathologist) that Phil probably had an undiagnosed learning disability that interfered with the processing of information — not something that affected his intelligence because it was clear he was very smart — but something that kept the information from organizing correctly as he heard it or tried to express it. I learned over time that he had struggled through school his entire life, and that eventually his frustrations turned into anger which led to a lot of fighting and negative behaviors. His dreams were even violent — recurring dreams of bears stalking him to kill him. He had felt like the whole world was against him and, in order to survive, he had to fight.

Sadly, it was true in a way. Many of his teachers thought he was a lost cause and did little to help (though, in their defense, little was known about learning disabilities then, so they weren't equipped with the knowledge that we have today). Phil graduated from high school but did not finish college. He was forced to find work and settle for jobs that were less than fulfilling, although he was blessed with good friends along the way.

By the time I met him, he was in his early thirties and working as a lineman for Arkansas Power and Light. He had learned to compensate and the pain he had gone through had grown his character.

I remember a particular evening after we were first married. We had been to a party at the home of a wealthy family in town. We were walking to the car in the dark, and it was very cold, so we were walking fast. I couldn't see Phil but knew he was right beside me. He chuckled quietly, and I asked him what he was laughing about. He said, "Oh, I was just thinking about how I was probably the only guy at the party who worked in the mud all day."

After I thought about it, I realized he was right. Every man there would have been considered a "white collar" professional. Only Phil was a "blue collar" worker and it didn't bother him a bit. His identity wasn't rooted in what he did and he didn't compare himself to others. He saw people on the same ground in which he saw himself — level. It was the thing I admired most about him and still do today. He's a special man and probably has no idea what a blessing he is to so many, especially to me.

I once heard a young man named Brooks Gibbs share part of his life experiences at a church function. He had learning disabilities growing up and experienced emotional hardships from the taunts he received from his peers for being different. He talked about his faith and how God had met him at his point of need and revealed His love for him at an early age, and then he said, "I have come to believe that those who have everything are the ones truly disabled." I have come to believe he was absolutely right.

My childhood experiences had been much different than Phil's. Learning came easily. Favor came easily. Opportunities abounded. It was my normal and I regret to say I took it for granted. Rather than growing in character, I grew in things that gave me a false identity and sense of security — layers of things that created an illusion as I looked at life.

The seeds of truth that had been planted over the course of my childhood by my parents, my grandparents, and Godly teachers, to some extent had remained dormant. A few seeds had sprouted into fruitful but small plants — nothing really breath-taking to speak of, and still others had been choked out by the weeds of the world. I wasn't really aware of the fact that my life was like a garden and my heart the soil in which my thoughts and actions were rooted. But it was, and it needed drastic cultivation. I married Phil when this "cultivation" began to happen. Over the past 18 years, I have been pruned countless times by the Master Gardener Himself.

I have felt a deep impression to share my story. I'm not sure why really. It is one of the hardest things I have ever attempted, and, because of that, have continually put it off. I don't want to do anything that would appear I was elevating myself or my experiences. All of us who recognize the authority of God upon our lives, and choose to live under it, have experiences worth sharing. They are like pathways that help to lead others safely across the pitfalls of life. In this way, our lives are like bridges, and, when we share them and the things that God has taught us through them, we are like bridge builders. I don't think for one minute that my life's story is more important than anyone else's, for I know I am no one. Yet, in some ways, I am everyone, and so are you.

Our mere existence as humans unites us and beckons not only a call to freedom but also a call to slavery in some form. We are bound by our needs, our ideas, our culture, comforts, and expectations — those we have for others and those we have for ourselves based on our ambitions, our abilities, our opportunities, our biases, and much more. All of these things, if given more leverage than they should have, will skew our perception of what really matters and result in a silent bondage that takes place almost without our knowledge. It seems that truth becomes so buried in the lies we are living that when we are actually faced with it from time to time, we either react in defense or respond by laughing at its simplistic short comings in answer to our complicated problems. However, our perceptions, regardless of what they are or how they came to be, don't change reality. Truth is truth. Discovering it, and our need for it, is life's greatest treasure and greater than any gift I could ever receive or give.

> You parents — if your children ask for a loaf of bread, do you give them a stone instead? Or if they ask for a fish, do you give them a snake? Of course not! So if you sinful people know how to give good gifts to your children, how much more will your heavenly Father give good gifts to those who ask him. (Matthew 7:9-11)

CHAPTER ONE
Poverty

Dedicated to mothers & those first born.
In honor of Jessica

God blesses those who are poor and realize their need for him, for the Kingdom of Heaven is theirs.
— Matthew 5:3

I always knew I would have a little girl and that she'd be just like an angel. I was right; I did, and she is.

We named her May Olivia. She is my first child by birth and only daughter. Her name is derived from family and Biblical history. "May" is my grandmother's name spelled differently. "Olivia" comes from the Mount of Olives where Jesus spent much time alone in prayer. To us, the name signified the strength of silence, oneness with God, and peace; the place Jesus retreated for solitude and prayer, and the place He will return. We think she is the epitome of her name.

I had no idea how that child would change my life. It was something inconceivable to someone who had never known motherhood. In almost an instant, she changed the way I saw the world. No longer did I think of things from my perspective. I thought of them from hers. I dreamed about her life and of the things I wanted to give to her and do with her. At times, I was even paralyzed with fear thinking of the things that could happen to her.

We had a house alarm system, two outdoor German Shepherd dogs, and a pipe fence along the perimeter of our five-acre piece of land complete with a security gate, and yet there were nights I couldn't sleep for fear someone would sneak in and take her. I feared the fire ants in the yard and the snakes that could be lurking in the flowerbeds. I was on top of her everywhere she went and couldn't enjoy anything without her. I was obsessed, overly protective, and head-over-heels in love with the most beautiful baby I had ever seen!

Despite my unhealthy obsessions and fears, she is developing into a lovely young lady. When I began writing this, Olivia was nine years old and finishing the fourth grade. Her face reflected a spirit of beauty with big blue eyes that seemed to speak all by themselves. She was kind and reserved, reflective and balanced — a "social butterfly" content wherever she was.

Today, Olivia is 13 and getting ready to enter high school. She's still a social butterfly but content mainly when she's on her phone or with her friends. Though she's a typical young teenage girl (with a typical young teenage girl attitude), she continues to demonstrate strong character. Her boldness impresses me and sometimes shocks me. I can see that she is a leader-in-the-making; one who will probably lead by example and with quiet strength.

Though Olivia reminds me of many colors, she mostly reminds me of blue — a sky blue that is clear, transparent, and refreshingly peaceful. She is pure and sees with her heart, not her eyes. When Olivia was a toddler and beginning to speak in sentences, I would make comments about things and often, on pretty days, would say, "God sure made a pretty day today!" Not long after, while driving to town one gray and cloudy day, this little voice spontaneously rose from the back of the car saying, "God sure made a pretty day, didn't He Mommy?" I was taken off guard. Her statement caught me right in the middle of what I will call "mental complaining." I wasn't happy at all by the weather and was wishing for something better. With eyes full of tears, I responded as best I could, "He sure did, Olivia. He sure did."

Because her soul seems timeless, there have been moments my expectations have been too high and I forgot she is just a young girl. Yet, what I have learned from her is grace because what I have experienced from her is grace. In all of my frailties and misgivings, she has never held anything against me or remembered a fault. She quickly forgives even when it is not requested and so far, she forgets. She is merciful and loving and already demonstrates a love for the young and vulnerable.

God used her to show me something that transformed my life that I never saw coming. Once it started, it snowballed. That something was Someone.

I am ashamed to admit that it wasn't until Olivia was born when I was 30 years old that I actually understood my need for a Savior. After all, I *am* a

Southern Baptist girl, raised in a loving, conservative, and traditional family with deep roots in small town America, and the Church.

At six years of age, I learned to water ski on the Ouachita River just south of the Crossett Bridge. I can still bait a hook (with a worm — I don't do crickets), and I am pretty good at shelling peas. As a teenager, I valued our party barge, fishing gear, and ski boat as much as I did my car and wardrobe.

I remember asking my grandmother one day why she and Granddaddy didn't build their house in a different neighborhood (one my young and immature mind thought was more suited to them because it had bigger houses and was closer to "the Club" where Granddaddy played golf every day). With her bright eyes and large smile, she responded without hesitation, "Well, my friends over there might not like it if I decided to shell peas on the front porch!" I knew she was teasing, but also knew she was probably right. Shelling peas on the porch and "country club" living didn't really go together, but somehow they did in her. My grandmother was always true to herself no matter where she was or who she was with — the same trait I see in my husband. It is a gift she and my granddaddy passed down and one I have treasured well into adulthood. They loved God. They loved people — rich or poor, black or white. And, they loved life — on the golf course, on the river, and on the front porch.

Their faith in God and their love for their family included their community. I believe the order of their priorities led to prosperity not only for them, but for those around them. The case is true for many in their generation, and in my opinion, that is why they are fittingly known as "The Greatest Generation." How I miss them.

Because my parents and grandparents were so grounded, I felt just as comfortable at the Country Club as I did on the river. My granddaddy was an oil man and my father a successful businessman so I was blessed, not only with love, but with opportunities. I received a public school education and later received degrees from a private college for women and a state university, so my educational experience, like my childhood experience, was fairly broad and diverse.

I grew up going to First Baptist Church. As I have heard my pastor, Dr. Matthew Pearson, say, "I began attending nine months before I was born." In fact, it's the only church to which I have ever belonged. Every time the doors opened at First Baptist, we were there. Seriously. We were. In many ways it was an extension of my home. I loved it and couldn't imagine my life without those in my family of faith. I still remember the many faces and events surrounding Sunday school, Vacation Bible School, Wednesday night

GA's and Acteens, and then later in junior high and high school, the many youth/mission trips, lock-ins, and fellowships. I knew all about Jesus and the main stories of the Bible. I could find most scriptures without using the Table of Contents. I was baptized and even rededicated my life, twice! So, with all of that good, wholesome upbringing, I couldn't help but wonder why it took me so long to get it?

> Other seeds fell on shallow soil with underlying rock. The seeds sprouted quickly because the soil was shallow. But the plants soon wilted under the hot sun, and since they didn't have deep roots, they died. (Matthew 13:5-6)

When I was in the tenth grade, I started dating someone who attended a church of a different denomination. It was the first time my world of religion was challenged by a different viewpoint. I was curious, so my boyfriend and I started meeting with a man from his church so that I could learn and understand the doctrine of this particular denomination. This started a discovery process that lasted for ten years. During this time I attended and explored several different denominations in search of the one that was right, assuming there was one that was right.

I was a sophomore in college during this 10-year period at which time I took a class called "Philosophy of Religion". Thinking it would be a class on the different religions of the world, I was surprised to find that it was instead a class that centered on the concept of God. Every argument we examined ended with "…therefore, God does not exist". To my shock and surprise, it made a lot of sense. I was dumbfounded like a deer caught in headlights and couldn't even come up with a logical defense though my heart emphatically disagreed with each conclusion. Never before had I questioned whether or not God existed because I knew in my heart He did. I had always loved Him, always prayed to Him, and searched for Him. All I wanted to know was which denominational doctrine was right about Him and was trying to figure that out, but THIS! This scared me and rocked me to the core of my being.

After attending the class for a couple of weeks, I couldn't take it any longer. I left class one morning, went straight to my dorm room, and called my parents, feeling sure they would let me drop it. I mean, why wouldn't they? The information I was hearing might persuade me to believe God wasn't real, and that's not what *they* believed. So I knew it wouldn't be a problem, or, at least, that's what I thought. To my surprise, they encouraged me to continue. It was the greatest gift they could have ever given me because it forced me to take ownership of my convictions by thinking them through.

At the end of the course, my faith in God Almighty was stronger than ever before. He is not reasonable but is, instead, beyond comprehension. That is why all logical arguments conclude He does not exist which in itself is confirmation that He does — they're *logical* arguments! We cannot understand Him (Isaiah 40:12-31).

There are truths that are relative to our individual preferences and there are truths that are absolute and never change regardless of who we are or what we think about them. My favorite meal is hot water cornbread, turnip greens with pepper sauce, and iced tea with lemon. That is the best meal I can think of and the truth as it relates to me. It is not the truth for many other people (probably *most* people). God, on the other hand, cannot be true relative to my preference. If He is, then He's not God. He's just a god — a counterfeit that I accept as true because I choose to believe it or because someone else says I should.

> *The trouble with the world is not that people know so little, but that they know so many things that ain't so.*
> *— Mark Twain*

I think in a deep sense I knew this was true at a young age and for whatever reason couldn't let it go until I worked things out. Just as Paul instructed the Church at Philippi, we all have to work out our salvation believing God will work in us to will and to act according to His good purpose (Philippians 2:12-13). I suppose that is why it took me so long to understand. There is so much information to consider. So many good, intelligent people who believe different things and so much pride that gets in the way because everyone thinks they're right. There have been so many times I just wanted to throw up my hands and forget it. But every time I started to do that, something would get my attention (a thought, a phrase…) and I would focus my efforts back on pursuing truth.

That was never any clearer than in those early days of motherhood. As an ordinary, American girl growing up in a small, southern town, God had always been a part of my life. As I stated before, I can't remember not loving Him or talking to Him. But, as much as I loved Him, I did not understand my need for a Savior. I knew about Jesus and I accepted what I knew, but when I look back over my teenage years and early adulthood, I did not make my decisions based on His guidance. My heart was not hidden in Him

(Colossians 3:3), and I certainly didn't live for Him. I lived for me and, for the most part, was pretty happy about it, that is, until a precious, newborn child came into my life and caught my attention.

All of a sudden I had a greater responsibility than ever before. This little thing that weighed barely six pounds was dependent on me for everything. I was overwhelmed by the blessing and the responsibility. I loved her with a love I had never experienced. It was deep and pure, and I knew in an instant I would give my life for her. And, that's when it hit me. I *would* die for her if it meant her life would be spared, but any such sacrifice on my part would only be a temporary gain for there is *"a time to be born and a time to die…"* for all of us (Ecclesiastes 3:2).

The love I felt for my little girl was an imperfect image of God's perfect love for me, of His love for all of humanity. His life through Jesus Christ is the light that shows us the way in this dark and limited world (John 1:4-5). His death was not just another death or a temporary fix. It was meaningful. It had eternal purpose. And, as a result, our lives, when placed under Him, also have purpose and meaning beyond what this world can offer.

Someone else did die for my daughter and that death did more than create a little extra time on earth for her. It created a stream in the desert; a stream of living water that gives *eternal* life (John 4:13-14). That was what I wanted for Olivia — life *forever*, at *home* with God, safe and sound, full and bright, happy and healthy, *always*. Where she went to school, what she would choose as a profession, who she married…all of those things paled in comparison to this. Nothing was more important than her relationship with God through Christ.

I had been blinded by a perception of life that prioritized family, friends, work, education, money, reputation, acceptance, popularity, prestige, comfort, power, and fun before God — and not just God, but God through the Person of Jesus Christ. My desire to be independent and my ability to achieve my personal goals — things that seemed good and are good with the right perspective — kept me separated from the light of His life.

I didn't realize it, but by exercising my right to myself without acknowledging the authority of God upon my life, I was walking in spiritual darkness, and it wasn't until I experienced the love and limited power of a mother for a child that I understood God's unfailing and perfect love for me. I saw who I was and understood that no matter how capable or self-sufficient, I could not come to God on my own. I could not guarantee eternal life for my precious child or guarantee her safety. I needed a Savior, and there could be only one. It was like a light had been turned on in my mind, and in a very real way it had.

Our lives can be so immersed in Biblical knowledge that we become desensitized to the Person of Christ and, therefore, fail to respond to Him on a personal level. In other words, we can know a lot *about* Jesus without really knowing Him, and if we don't know Him, we can't understand who we are. All of the motions we go through to be good Christians and live out the Christian life can be achieved without participating in a personal relationship with the One who *is* Christianity. Until we see Him and understand our need for Him, we don't see ourselves.

The birth of Olivia, my first child, enabled me to see my poverty and understand the absolute truth of Jesus Christ, my Savior and my God. From that moment on I wanted nothing to ever come between Him and me or my prayers and His ear on behalf of those I love (James 5:16; Proverbs 15:29). That desire gave me the courage to turn away from the things I wanted and turn toward Him. I began to pray for God to change me, to teach me His ways and truths, and to show me more and more of who He is. Though I knew I had much to learn (and had no idea how much I would have to *unlearn*), I knew in my heart He could be trusted. That, I was sure was an absolute truth and an anchor for my soul that would hold (Hebrews 6:19).

> Show me your ways, O LORD, teach me your paths; guide me in your truth and teach me, for you are God my Savior, and my hope is in you all day long. (Psalm 25:4-5 NIV)

CHAPTER TWO
Fearless

Dedicated to Fathers and "Children of Thunder"

Such love has no fear, because perfect love expels all fear.
—1 John 4:18

"Am I going to heaven?"

"Yes, you are," I replied.

"Are you sure?"

Looking intently into the eyes of my 6-year-old son John, who I believed was not ready to process the concept of salvation at that time and stood on a stool facing me across the kitchen island, I answered as cool and confidently as I could with a nod, "Uh huh".

"What if I say bad words?"

"Yep," I said matter-of-factly.

"What if I smoke?" John asked, this time with a squint of one eye and a testing glance.

"Well, Papa smoked, and I know he's in heaven," I replied moving next to him on the other side of the isle.

"Will you go to heaven before me?"

Oh, my, we're getting serious, I thought. "I don't know the answer to that, John."

"I hope not," he said with a weak, toothless smile.

"Well, if I do," I replied trying to keep things as light as possible, "I'll sure be waiting on you when you get there!"

"But, what would happen to me and Livvy and Sam if you and daddy BOTH went to heaven at the same time before we did?"

Trying not to reveal my concern for his fears or how impressed I was with the depth of his thinking, I said with a confident smile, "I guess you guys would get to live with one of your great aunts and uncles. Either way, you would be very loved and cared for, John, but you don't need to think about that. We trust God with your life, and He will take care of you no matter what happens."

As the conversation turned back toward more comfortable things, I silently marveled over John's keen insight but was concerned for the fears it revealed. *"He's just like me,"* I thought. His thoughts revealed the same fears I had as a teenager, but at a much younger age.

John is my second child and only son by birth. I always think of him when I see the color orange. He has a vibrant personality and tons of energy — a real if-you-can-walk-you-might-as-well-run kind of guy. He has a ready smile and laughs out loud with no inhibition. John is witty, transparent, persistent, and *a bit* mischievous.

One day, after having his promised one sip of Coke from my glass, John kept trying to reach for the glass to get more. I said, "John, I have to be able to trust you. You promised to drink just one sip and be done." Without a blink, John grabbed the glass again, looked me straight in the eye, and said with great persuasion, "Trust me one more time!"

Though he is charming, John is also brutally honest — which can be *not so charming* at times and frankly, catches me off guard often. Unlike his sister, I'm afraid empathy is something he will have to learn the hard way.

This was pretty obvious when in four-year-old preschool, he got in trouble for telling another child he had ugly eyes. When asked why he said this, John shrugged his shoulders and very matter-of-factly stated, "Because he does." Having entered into the process of adopting our third child from China by that time, I couldn't help but wonder what John's perception of his new brother would be. Deep down I knew his little brother would help him grow in his sensitivity toward others, but I had no idea how much.

I always felt in my heart I would have a little girl, and somehow I always had a deep feeling at least one of my children would come to me through adoption, but the thought of a son — by birth or adoption — was an unfamiliar thought. Regardless of why, finding out I was carrying a little boy in my second pregnancy was a delightful surprise with which I was unsure how to handle. Strangely, I could "see" Olivia before she was born, but I could not envision this baby boy even though he was growing inside me.

Already things were different. During my pregnancy with Olivia, my body stayed pretty well in proportion. She moved very little — just enough to let me know she was there, like a lady. John, on the other hand, kept me up and even woke me up with his rolling and tossing and turning around. Sometimes, it seemed like he was trying to kick his way out! It was no dainty or soft baby-like push either. It was hard and aggressive. My body definitely did not stay in proportion and to this day is not the same.

By my ninth month of pregnancy we still had not settled on a name. "John" was the name of choice, but it didn't sound like a baby's name. How could I call a baby a strong name like "John"? After a lot of prayer and deliberation, we settled on John Kinard — an even more masculine name that carried both Biblical and family heritage, things that were important to us.

When he was born, we called him "Baby John." Then, when he was two years old, his Sunday school teacher informed me he was no longer a baby and it became "John-John." Now, it's just lovingly "John" or sometimes "JOHN!" depending on the circumstances of the moment.

He has long hair (well, longer than most boys), big hazel-green eyes, and has been mistaken for a girl more than a few times. He's very cool in a natural way but sensitive and high maintenance with volatile and intense emotions. When he's happy, he's *really* happy, which, fortunately, is most of the time. When he's sad, he's heartbroken, and when he's mad, he's a downright handful!

Through all of this, John has taught me patience. Well, let me rephrase that; he has taught me how much I *need* patience — I'm still working on the acquisition. He has taught me the importance of integrity; of doing what I say I'm going to do and being who I say I am. And, honestly he has taught me that it is impossible. Time after time, I just seem to fail, but the pressure of accountability to my son has given me a desire *not* to fail and made me a better person.

John's candid questions about death and his demanding temperament brought my deepest fears to the surface and forced me to search for answers regarding something I was too scared to deal with on my own initiative. Through him God taught me more about myself and revealed more about who He is just as I had been asking Him to do from that first moment I realized how poor (and at the same time how rich) I was as I looked into the face of my first-born child.

Sadness discolors everything; it leaves all objects charmless...[1]

As a teenager, I hated New Year's Eve. As many people do, friends would plan parties and anxiously anticipate the celebration of a new year, but

I always dreaded it and usually went to bed early. Every New Year moved me closer to the time my life would change and I knew in my heart that change would not be welcome. I held deep fears about death and knew one day it would darken my door. Regardless of how hard I tried to ignore it, those fears were always there and eventually would come true.

One day short of my four-month wedding anniversary, my dad died from a sudden heart attack. I was 27 years old but might as well have been seven. I had no idea how to process what had happened. I couldn't. This happened three years before I understood my need for Jesus and what His life meant for those who trusted Him as Savior (those like my dad), so my heart was not only full of grief and sorrow but real fear and confusion. I didn't know where he was and couldn't place him anywhere that gave me peace.

Now, this was a strange thing for someone who loved God and had attended church all of her life. I knew I should have a better understanding, but the truth was I didn't, and I was too embarrassed to say otherwise. At that time, the reason didn't matter. All I knew was that my life had been turned inside out, and I needed help.

During the first few days, people came to support my mother and our family; people who loved my father and were very saddened by his death. One of my good friends came up to me during that time. I was in the kitchen getting some coffee when he approached with reluctance not really knowing what to say.

"Jennifer," he said, "I didn't want to come here today, and I don't know what to say except that I know your dad is in a better place."

I could barely respond and came out with a weak, "I guess."

It was so awkward and I was so confused. My father's death is what I feared the most and it happened just like I knew it would. Everything I had known and much of what gave me security, even at a mature age, changed in a moment.

It was as if the world changed colors right before my eyes. What seemed so bright and vivid became muted and dull. I could no longer place my father within the physical scope of daily life, and those places that had held him physically like his truck, his office, and his chair suddenly held no meaning. His soul wasn't there to fill them. The person who gave me my identity and who I depended on the most in this world had vanished.

I thought he was invincible. I *knew* he wasn't, but I still hoped somehow he was. He was a great man with deep faith and strong character. He was humble in heart, gentle in spirit, deliberate in his decisions, careful in word. He was respected, kind and always considerate; a gentleman who left us (what I thought was) way too soon.

To lessen the load of responsibilities and quite possibly the pain, my mother decided to sell not only the business that carried my dad's name and reputation, but she also decided to sell some personal properties that had been a part of my life from childhood. The void was overwhelming. I felt like I was being sucked into a vacuum where nothing was certain and trying desperately to find something to hold onto.

It was a hard time, and it took a long time to work through my grief. Just as I had ignored my fears by avoiding the turn of each New Year, I ignored my pain by throwing myself into the busyness of work.

In exactly three years Phil and I built a house, started two businesses, and had our first child (Olivia), while we both worked full-time and actively participated in programs at our church. It was pretty ridiculous but necessary for my survival. It was also very hard on our marriage. I turned to Phil for the same stability my dad had provided which was completely unfair and hurtful.

I remember taking walks soon after my dad passed away. It was the month of October and the fall weather was wonderful. Usually, on days such as those, I would be moved by the beauty, especially by the wind blowing through the trees and the visual contrast between their green tops and the azure blue sky — one of my favorite viewpoints of life. But, in those dark days, it didn't matter how beautiful things were on the outside. The sadness in my heart and the void in my life caused a disconnection. Though I could see the beauty, I couldn't feel it, not for a long time.

The trauma caused me to question what I believed. I wasn't sure of anything. I was supposed to be sure but wasn't, and deep down was very disturbed. Had I loved my dad *too much*? Did God take him out of my life because he meant too much to me?

These were questions that haunted me for many years; fears ignored and pushed into the dark recesses of my mind and almost forgotten until eleven years later when through the mouth of a babe, John's questions shed light on them.

I was so shaken by my conversation with John. I wanted to pray about it, but I was too scared to face it, too afraid John's fears were true just like mine had been. You see, when my father died, my childhood fears were realized; therefore, I concluded they must have been true. It was like the past was repeating itself, and since the thing I had been most afraid of had come true, I figured John's probably would too. Either Phil and/or I was going to die or John was because I loved him too much. I could barely breathe.

> Do not hide from your fear or pretend it isn't there. Anxiety that you hide in the recesses of your heart will give birth to fear of fear: a monstrous stepchild. Bring your anxieties out into the Light of My Presence, where we can deal with them together. Concentrate on trusting Me, and fearfulness will gradually lose its foothold within you.[2]

By this time, I did have a close relationship with God through Christ and was searching the Bible every day at length for more and more knowledge. Sometimes, twice a day, early and late, I would sit in the shady corner of my front porch or in the big leather chair in the den to study and pray; to learn more about Him and this love He had revealed to me several years earlier when Olivia was born.

Since then, God had been faithfully showing me His ways and teaching me His truths just as I had asked Him. Though I knew the Bible was a source for historical knowledge and divine truths, I discovered I could hear God's voice and understand His words to me as I read it with an open heart. The more I read, the more I wanted to read. I could hardly wait until the next morning when I could get up early and spend time with Him before the day began. I had learned *so much* over the past nine years about God, and because of that, I was a different person altogether.

So, as my habit was, I sat down to read the morning after my disturbing conversation with John. It was April 26, and to my amazement, it was apparently time for me to learn something about myself and to *unlearn* something about God. In *My Utmost for His Highest*, author Oswald Chambers laid out the story of Abraham's belief that he was to sacrifice his son.

> *Take now your son…and offer him…as a burnt offering on one of the mountains of which I shall tell you. (Genesis 22:2 NIV)*

Character determines how a man interprets God's will (cf. Psalm 18:25-26). Abraham interpreted God's command to mean that he had to kill his son, and he could only leave this tradition behind by the pain of a tremendous ordeal. God could purify his faith in no other way. If we obey what God says according to our sincere belief, God will break us from those traditions that misrepresent Him. There are many such beliefs to rid of, e.g., that God removes a child because the mother loves him too much (a devil's lie!) and, a travesty of the true nature of God. If the devil can hinder us from taking the supreme climb and getting rid of wrong traditions about God, he will do so; but if we keep true to God, God will take us through an ordeal which will bring us out into a better knowledge of Himself.[3]

No one, at any age, is ever ready to let go of a loving father or even the dream of one. There's a reason for that; they are made in the image of THE loving Father. Naturally, we are drawn to them and depend on them. What a great blessing to have such a strong and positive influence in one's life.

The death of my earthly father began a process of learning and unlearning, of removing beliefs that created a false perception of God (keeping me in bondage), and replacing them with truth. By remaining true to God when faced with my deepest fears, He was able to purify my faith through His Word, through the examples of Abraham and Isaac, and through the words of His servant generations later, Oswald Chambers. It was a lesson I will never forget.

I was standing on my front porch that morning facing the Sycamore trees that reminded me so much of my dad (they were his favorite trees). It was a beautiful morning. The breeze was cool. The air was crisp and the tops of the trees were swaying in the wind — their green tops a beautiful contrast against the morning sky — still one of my favorite viewpoints of life.

I realized then that, as extraordinary as my dad was, he was just a man. He was a sinner and he struggled with issues just like the rest of us. He died because he had a disease which smoking and stress exacerbated, not because I loved him too much. I couldn't see that because I didn't look at him through the image of God. Rather, I looked at God through the image of my dad. The process of disillusionment was painful but a marvelous gift I didn't even realize I needed.

> Many of the things in life that inflict the greatest injury, grief, or pain, stem from the fact that we suffer from illusions. We are not true to one another as facts, seeing each other as we really are; we are only true to our misconceived ideas of one another...There is only one Being who can completely satisfy to the absolute depth of the hurting human heart, and that is the Lord Jesus Christ.[4]

Although it took nine years for me to work through my grief, God was very patient, as He always is, and allowed me to learn at my own pace while guiding my course. Already He had taken His place in my life as my Savior a few years earlier and now was moving little by little, closer and closer to His rightful place in my life as my Father, my Protector and my Provider.

All along, He knew my needs and spoke to me in a way I could hear and understand. He does the same for all of His children. I am no exception for He shows no favoritism and died for all that we may have life (James 2:17, 1 Timothy 2:3-6).

Life — that's what I wanted for John, in all of its fullness; therefore, the iniquity of fear had to stop that day with me. So, with tears and trembling, I held my hand open and gave God my son. Only God is who He says He is. Only He is able to do what He says He will do. Regardless of my fears or determination, my good intentions or mistakes, God is always good, always present, always faithful, and more real than anything I can see, hear, touch, or even imagine. He is the Perfect Father, and His Word is true and alive, waiting to teach, waiting to comfort, and waiting to live through those who believe.

Today, my little "son of thunder" is ten years old and as bold in his convictions as was John the Baptist. God has gifted him with the ability to think critically beyond his years along with an eclectic personality and strong will. He was born to lead and I imagine will do so a bit more loudly than his sister. As he grows, I feel sure he's going to grow me too and probably make me a little nervous in the process. My prayer is that he will see me through the eyes of his Father and choose Him over all else; walking fearlessly and with confidence in the assurance of His unfailing love.

> In the beginning… The Word gave life to everything that was created, and his life brought light to everyone. The light shines in the darkness, and the darkness can never extinguish it. (John 1:1-5)

Notes
[1] L.B. Cowman, *Streams in the Desert* (The Zondervan Corporation, 1996), 306.
[2] Sarah Young, *Jesus Calling* (Thomas Nelson: Thomas Nelson, Inc., 2011), 210.
[3] Oswald Chambers, *My Utmost for His Highest* (Oswald Chambers Publication Association, Ltd. 1992), April 26.
[4] Ibid., July 30.

CHAPTER THREE
One Expectation

Dedicated to Children "born" by Adoption and their Forever Families

> *My soul, wait thou only upon God;*
> *for my expectation is from him.*
> *— Psalm 62:5 KJV*

Conception is a miraculous thing. Olivia and John were both tiny miracles — conceived after some minor medical intervention. I had always dreamed of four children (I still do even now), and was ecstatic when I learned I was pregnant with my third child.

I felt in my heart the baby was a girl, and I secretly named her Faith. I could see her already in my mind, but I was so busy caring for Olivia and John, now ages four and one, and working full-time in a fairly new job at my church, I hardly had time to dream about her.

She was due to arrive in January, 2004, but she never made it…well, she or *he*. The dream of that life died during one of the first routine check-ups when, at nine weeks, there was no heartbeat.

It took a while for the fact to sink in that there would be no sweet baby coming home at the first of the New Year. I went through the normal emotions of grief but strangely felt a peace throughout. Little did I know there was a precious child growing in the womb of an Asian woman on the other side of the world who would be coming home with us at the first of the New Year *almost exactly two years later.*

That Asian child was my son, Sam. He was born in February, 2004, one month later than the expected arrival of our third biological child.

We didn't meet him until January, 2006 and obtained legal custody the next day. He is my baby. He was four years old when I began to write these words and had been home with us a little over a year. Though I didn't give birth to him physically, he was born to us.

Sam reminds me the most of the color yellow. He is very happy and content, intelligent and kind — a precious child who is sensitive to his surroundings, gentle in spirit, observant, inquisitive, artistic, and very funny. Little gets by him. In fact, it has become a common thing in our family to consult Sam if anyone of us has misplaced something.

It started with the normal way of asking questions in general. Phil would say, "Has anyone seen my keys?" And, this little voice from another room would answer, "They're on the dining room table." After that happened several times with several different items, we quickly learned to go directly to the source of information. Now, it's "Sam, have you seen…?" Or Phil, Olivia, John and I will ask one another, "Where's Sam? I can't find…" And, nine times out of ten, he has the answer we're looking for.

He is fascinated with details, creating, dissecting, putting things together, and food. He easily entertains himself and could truly be addicted to video games. That boy can focus on something for hours, and he's a wealth of information — always wanting to know answers to questions that have never crossed my mind. For example, when he was five years old, I was tucking him into bed when he asked out of the blue, "Momma, when I get my resurrected body and fall down, will I bleed?" My responses to his questions usually entail part of an answer based on limited knowledge and then I end with, "but I'm not really sure; we'll have to research that."

Just the other day as we were walking from Sunday school to the sanctuary for the worship service, Sam asked me (again — out of the blue), "Momma, how do you make hydrogen peroxide?" As I hesitated (while frantically trying to remember my lessons from chemistry to prove I did know *something*), Sam said, "I know, I know…we'll have to Google it!"

Because he is genetically of Chinese descent, he is easily noticed and draws the attention of others everywhere we go. In a way, he's like a little yellow flower blooming among the grass that catches the eye and brings a smile. It's nice, and although we all celebrate Sam's heritage, there are times we all, including Sam, long to just be "normal" and unnoticed.

This was particularly hard on John. Being only a year and nine months older than Sam, he lost his place in our family as the baby boy overnight. He handled that with genuine grace and accepted his baby brother with an open heart, but the attention that Sam drew from people in public was the hardest.

It wasn't that Sam got more attention; Sam got *all* the attention. There were times people didn't even seem to notice John for he was just like another green blade of grass among many.

It was harder than I thought it would be. Sam wanted to blend in. John wanted to be noticed and became insecure when he was overlooked, and the momma bear in me wanted to roar over the situation a few times, but all in all, it was a time of character building in both boys. Sam and John both, over time, learned that their worth and their identity wasn't defined by how people responded or what they thought. It was defined by the One who made them each uniquely special and placed them together in life as brothers. We all learned and had to accept that we *were* different and that people are naturally curious and for the most part really care. We learned how to forgive and look past insensitivities that were not intentional or meant to harm. We all grew. I think the word for it is *grace*.

As I wrote this, Sam was sitting on the floor next to me working a floor puzzle. He was recovering from surgery four days earlier, which was the beginning of what will be a long process for him. He was born with bilateral cleft lip and palate meaning his face didn't form correctly before birth leaving him with an open space in the center of his top lip all the way back through the top of his mouth. Because of it, the bone that holds his top teeth did not form and will have to be structured surgically. It affects his physical appearance, his speech, his breathing, and his sleep.

As I sat with him following surgery rubbing his swollen feet and looking at his puffy little face, I was overwhelmed with gratitude for the opportunity to love Sam and to care for him, and I grieved for the days lost when he was a little baby and I didn't get to hold him and tell him how much he was loved. How I wished I could have been there for him, but God took care of his needs through a loving foster family, and I was grateful for that and the time I had now been given. In a way, Sam's life has impacted three mothers and families — two we may never know fully how, but, without a doubt his memory will live in their hearts always…and they in our prayers. When I told Sam, "I am so glad I get to take care of you," he replied very simply with a smile on his face, "You're welcome."

So often, people tell us how much we have blessed Sam, and we know this is true, but what they don't understand is that we are equally blessed by him and perhaps even more so. As Christians, we are all called to care for the vulnerable, but the way we do that depends upon God's unique design in each of us. Adoption is a special blessing that many times comes to families and orphaned children out of sorrow, but when we seek God and allow

Him, He takes all of our circumstances — our joys and disappointments, our sorrows and sufferings — and brings goodness out of them. He does this because He is all knowing and all powerful and all loving, and His promise of love is to *work all things together for good for those who love Him* (Romans 8:28). We are a family, an adoptive family — Plan A — because in God's design there is no other plan.

> Take delight in the LORD, and he will give you your heart's desires. (Psalm 37:4)

When Phil and I first married, our hearts were drawn toward adoption. The first thing we did was request information from a well-known, Christian adoption agency. I remember being so excited to receive the application packet and took it with me to begin filling out during my lunch hour. I will never forget coming to a form that clearly stated in black and white that it was mandatory for us to sign before our application would even be considered. It was a Pro Life statement.

I was 27 years old at the time (same year Phil and I married and my dad passed away) and I didn't really have an opinion on the subject. Personally, I didn't think I could ever go through with an abortion though I had a few friends who had. I couldn't express a viewpoint and certainly couldn't defend one. I simply had never thought about it that much because it wasn't something that affected me. What I did know was that there was something deeply wrong with the requirement to sign this form before the organization would open up their doors (and their hearts) to us and what God was calling us to do.

The whole application went in the trash, and we began to pray over the next days and weeks for direction. God led us to another organization; a smaller one, but well-known and well-respected. They were not known as a Christian organization and did not market themselves as such, but it didn't take long for us to understand they were driven by their Christian faith, organized, and doing Kingdom work through humanitarian services for orphaned children. I learned then that organizations aren't Christians; people are Christians. There is a vast difference. The minute we lose sight of this, I believe we strangle the life of Christ in us, eventually snuffing out His love and mercy and grace through our attempts to institutionalize our beliefs and control others.

That incident was a blessing in disguise because it was the spark to a stent of prayerful research and study that helped me think through polarizing issues until I understood their controversies and was confident in my position. Knowing my position and why I hold that position is important. Standing in that position is important, but holding it over someone else as a requirement for acceptance or friendship is not.

The moment I spoke on the phone to the Arkansas coordinator of this international adoption agency I knew God would direct us through her. She was real, and God did use her to help us, but not immediately. Phil and I completed paperwork and attended a workshop, but then we hesitated when the next step meant no turning back. It wasn't that we were afraid. We just felt a restraint and backed off. For a reason we didn't understand, it just wasn't time.

Fast forward ten years and two children later, the "call" came again. This time, we were in California at a children's ministry conference at Saddleback Church. The children's pastor shared the story of his daughter through adoption and then he made a statement very similar to this, "Adoption is not a human desire; it is a God desire. If you have the desire to adopt, it is not just a good idea. It is a call." My heart nearly stopped!

We were at a crossroads. To be completely honest, I was at a crossroads, but I wasn't sure where Phil was. A lot was going on in our lives. Olivia and John were then five and two. Phil was working a new job after the sale of our downtown restaurant and coffee bar, and I had just surrendered my life to God's work through the children's ministry during that week at Saddleback, something that surprised me but I was very sure and excited about.

Phil and I didn't talk about what we heard until after we were on our way home. Our flight to Little Rock had been cancelled, so we decided to fly to Dallas and rent a car to get us from there to the Little Rock Airport where we had left our car. We were listening to the radio and an advertisement for international adoption came on. It broke the ice and gave me enough courage to broach the subject.

By the time we got home, it was in the early hours of the morning and we were exhausted. We lived in a beautiful two-story home; one we had built several years earlier. It was part of my flurry of projects when I was in "survival mode" after my dad passed away. I envisioned us living there when our grandchildren came to see us. It was our forever home — our dream home that rested on five acres just outside of city limits.

My favorite part of the home was the line of Sycamore trees that ran between the driveway and the house. I can't count how many days I gazed at those beautiful trees as they moved in the wind. They were located on the west side of the house, so I could see them out the kitchen windows.

For several years I prepared dinner for my family while watching Phil play with the kids in the large grassy area on the other side of those trees against the setting sun. It is forever etched in my mind — them on the earth and God in the sky; His brilliant array of colors and light over them, over us as the night drew near.

It brings tears to my eyes thinking about it. I thought we'd be there for the rest of our lives, and, in a way, I guess we will be as I ponder moments like those time after time in my mind. The memories are deeply sweet and lined with a little sadness, but it's enough.

When we walked in the door and through the kitchen to the den early that morning, something very strange happened. It was dark, and the moon was shining through the windows, so we could see pretty well.

It was as if I was seeing my home from someone else's eyes. I looked around amazed at the beauty and the size of our home. I was in awe, but I was also confused. I couldn't believe what I was seeing. Phil was experiencing the exact same thing. As if a veil had been removed from our eyes so that we could see more clearly, we saw our home from a whole new perspective.

When we got to our bedroom, we didn't know what to say. It was obviously a gift that enabled us both to see our lives from the outside in and gave us absolute assurance God's timing was now. We had no reason NOT to adopt, and now understood just how much we had to share, but we had no idea where to start. That's when Kimberly, the adoption coordinator who was "real," came back into our lives.

We called the agency we had become familiar with ten years earlier and got the ball rolling. Almost immediately we had to choose a country. A country! How do you choose a country? We were tempted to start with convenience; the shortest distance, the shortest length of stay and the least expensive, but we knew that wasn't right, so we carefully looked at the criteria for each country and determined what was in our comfort zone and what was not. China was out because we really didn't want to fly half way around the world and stay for two weeks. Russia was out because that trip was five weeks. Guatemala, now that trip was only three days. That looked pretty enticing...

Then Kimberly asked this question, "When you think about your child through adoption, what do you see when you close your eyes?"

Well, I had to admit the answer was an Asian girl — that's what we both saw, and with Kimberly's encouragement, that's the country we chose.

We named our little Asian girl Ava. I couldn't wait to see a picture of her! We talked to Olivia and John about Ava, Ava this, and Ava that. Then one day I received an email from the agency asking us to review information on a waiting child. The email stated that there had been 13 children on the waiting child list and all had found their forever families *except for one.*

I opened the files and saw a picture of a two-year-old little boy with a shaved head and no smile standing in a parking lot wearing a blue striped shirt and red shoes. He was holding a banana and wasn't even looking at the camera. His name was Ning Fu Zhan. He was born with bilateral cleft lip and palate and was ready for adoption. I said a silent prayer for him and then closed the file. I was pretty sure this was not our child, but, out of courtesy mainly, responded to the email by asking that we be notified if he had not found his forever family after one month's time. I figured we would never hear about this little boy again and felt sure God would work it all out for him.

One month went by before another email was received. Ning Fu Zhan had not found his forever family. We were faced with a choice we had not anticipated; another crossroads, but this time the way wasn't as clear.

We never put anything down about a boy. We were seeking a girl — a baby girl; like the one in my dreams that never came home. The one I saw when I closed my eyes — Ava, who had no medical issues. Not a boy or a toddler who had major medical issues. He wasn't even smiling in his picture. I kept trying to see a glimpse of his personality in some other pictures we received later, but I couldn't tell anything. I didn't see a spark. I didn't feel a spark. The situation wasn't what I had dreamed about, and, yet, here we were. There he was. What were we supposed to do?

I guess I kept waiting to *feel* something. My heart went out to the little boy in the picture. I knew he was well cared for and loved by his foster family, which was an unusual setting for an orphaned child in China. He just wasn't what we had envisioned. In fact, he was the opposite!

Then the thought came to me as if God was speaking Himself, *"You have followed me now for seven years. You understand my love for you and for all of my children* (Jeremiah 103:11). *You know you can trust Me; that My Word is true and My plans are good* (Psalm 29:11). *Knowing these things, do you think I would allow this child to come to your attention without it being my desire? Would I try to confuse you? Of course not* (1 John 2:27)*! This is your child. It doesn't matter how you feel. The feelings will come. It only matters that you trust me and follow my direction."*

Six months later (and a year and a half after our "unveiling of the eyes" experience), Phil and I left for China. It was January 2007. Everything was fine until it came time to board the international flight from Chicago to our first stop in Seoul, Korea. That's when I started to panic. I was leaving everything I knew, everything I loved, to fly to the other side of the world for a child I had never laid eyes on and whose personality I couldn't even get a glimpse of because he wasn't even smiling in his picture! Now, usually, I am in a fair amount of control, but I was starting to lose it. It was midnight and time to go. I had never been so scared in my entire life!

You need to know that I was also exhausted. After surrendering to the children's ministry during that same time we heard God's call to extend our family through adoption at Saddleback Church, things drastically changed with my work. I thought when I surrendered to the children's ministry that meant I would work *in the children's ministry* within the walls of the church for a long time. Fourteen years was what had been suggested as an optimal time in one place for that kind of ministry and it made sense to me. I was ready and had a plan. It takes time to build a ministry that deliberately and effectively disciples children.

Instead, that decision led to the start-up of a nonprofit humanitarian organization (one of those "faith-driven" ones) that served children with developmental differences. It was another situation I never saw coming that hit me in the face and drove me to my knees. Apparently, I had a lot to learn and I needed to learn fast. So as my Father did best, He had cut straight to the chaise.

Within one month after returning home from that life-changing trip, I started meeting with four women who became cofounders of what is now known as HOPE Landing. We started meeting after work and discussed and planned late into the evening. Our plan was to establish an organization that served children with developmental differences from a holistic standpoint, meeting basic physical and intellectual needs as well as emotional, social, and spiritual needs; a place that met needs of their families and worked with others, bringing people together and filling a void in our community. Never did I think I would be the one leading it. I didn't *want* to lead it. I didn't know a thing about running a nonprofit, much less starting one from the ground up. It was ridiculously crazy.

After three months, we were incorporated in the State of Arkansas, and by seven months the organization owned an 80-acre ranch just five miles east of town. Someone had to quit their job and lead, and because of the circumstances God had allowed, the only one who was able to do that was me. So, by the time we were in the Chicago airport getting ready to leave for China, I had been working for a full year in this new capacity. I was not emotionally prepared for what was happening. I hadn't had time to really process it, and it was all hitting home in that terminal at midnight.

That's when Phil made a bold move that probably saved my sanity — and his. He upgraded our tickets to Business Class. I didn't know at the time how much it cost, I just knew the trip was going to be a little easier, and that (along with the thought of our son expecting us) gave me enough courage to board the plane.

As I boarded, I was trying very hard not to hyperventilate. Every step was deliberate and slow. I felt like I was in a time warp. When I stepped onto the plane, I looked to my right and saw the huge expanse of seats and people getting settled in for the trip. I started to go in when the stewardess motioned toward a stairway.

Not knowing there was an upstairs, my fear lessened to a cautious curiosity as I thought, "Okay, that's kind of cool." As I entered the second story of the plane, it was like entering a different world. To my delight, the space was dimly lit and cozy with enough room to move around easily. I could hear soft, classical music and the stewardesses were sweet and polite. I was in heaven! My spirit lifted immediately and though I was still very sad to leave all that I knew and loved, I was encouraged and slept nearly eight hours. It was a pointed reminder my Father would never give me more than I could handle (Matthew 11:28-30). Because of His tender care through my loving husband, I was rested and emotionally ready for the days ahead.

> Now our knowledge is partial and incomplete… (1 Corinthians 13:9)

We flew eight times during our 15-day trip. It was on the third flight, the one that took us to Nanning City in the province of Guangxi in the southern part of China where our son lived, that we finally decided on a name.

Both Olivia and John had family names from their earthly and spiritual heritage. It would be the same for Fu Zhan or "Zhan Zhan" as we were told he was often called by his foster family. In English, it would likely be pronounced as "John John." That was interesting.

I had been reading from my Bible almost every waking minute I was seated. It was the only way I could keep my mind off my worries and stay calm. We thought about keeping part of his Chinese name, but the impression that felt strongest was on an entirely new name. We decided on Samuel James. Samuel was a family name, and it was also the name of God's servant, the prophet, who was adopted and raised by Eli, the priest, as his mother promised the Lord if He would only give her a child.

Samuel heard the voice of God when he was a young child and he responded. That was a good name to have. James was the brother of John (and I suspected my James and John would be two peas in a pod), but there was also another James who was the half-brother of Jesus. The book of James is my favorite book in the Bible, so...Samuel James it was.

Sam was found by police at a gas station in a poor area. He had not been there for very long. Because of the medical needs surrounding his cleft lip and palate, he was placed in a foster home prior to six months of age where he remained until the day we came for him.

I'd never been so nervous in my life! I literally thought I was going to throw up before I got to the room where he was waiting. When we walked in, he was sitting on a rocking toy playing with a cell phone while his foster father knelt down close to him. He was beautiful! We took pictures and gave gifts to him and to his foster father, who smiled sweetly as he spoke gently and lovingly to Sam. He seemed to really love our little boy. Sam never smiled but took everything in. He was polite but distant. When it was time to go, the separation was quick but traumatic.

After an initial emotional outburst, Sam pretty much shut down except for the times he would stand at the door of the hotel room and call out for "Ma Ma!" until he was so exhausted that he just hung his little head and sobbed. It broke our hearts. He couldn't be comforted — certainly not by us.

Close to three days after Sam became legally ours, he was sitting on the floor of the hotel room in front of the bed exhausted from crying. We had done all we could to distract his attention with toys and food, but he was still heart-broken and scared. I had given Sam a small photo album with pictures of Olivia and John, our house and rooms in our house, and our dogs. These were things he would see and recognize immediately when we got home. I remembered Sam's foster father giving me some pictures, so I found them and placed them in the photo album with the others. Sam took the album and held it close to his face, studying every picture closely as he flipped from one to the other and back again. After about ten minutes of this intense focus, he slammed down the photo album, got up, and started playing. It was amazing — like a fog had been lifted. We were so relieved.

Soon after that, our first exchange of communication and his first real smile centered around food. Phil did a thumbs-up, and from that moment on, all throughout our meals, it was thumbs-up with a big smile and later adding a tap of the glasses to celebrate whatever we were drinking. Little by little he started to trust us, and by the time we traveled home, his little hand was a fixture around my finger.

Our beautiful, brown-skinned, almond-eyed, curly headed little boy (yes, curly!!) was amazing and fit into our family as if he was born to us, but that's just it — he *was* born to us. God had a plan all along and guided our thoughts and our steps to keep us in tune and in time with Him so that through the hoops of humanity, He could bring to fruition something holy and divine.

I marvel at the way God brought Sam into our lives and shudder to think that I could have missed it just because he didn't fit my expectations. If we had said no to the picture of the boy who wasn't smiling (because we were saying yes to the picture we created in our minds), we — all of us — would have missed one of the greatest blessings in our lives.

Sam *exceeded* our expectations just as Olivia and John had. Through his little life, I learned that only God is my true expectation. Everything my heart longs for, lies in Him, and He will bring it to pass if only I will trust His love and accept His authority over me. He is Love and He is the Authority whether I accept it or not, but the gift He has given me to choose according to my own free will, allows me to bless Him (and be blessed by Him) by reciprocating His love and by choosing to live under His direction and care. Without Him, I am also an orphaned child, but with Him, I am a part of a beautiful adoptive family — a forever family — that nothing, not even death, can separate (Romans 8:38-39).

> Even before he made the world, God loved us and chose us in Christ to be holy and without fault in his eyes. God decided in advance to adopt us into his own family by bringing us to himself through Jesus Christ. This is what he wanted to do, and it gave him great pleasure. (Ephesians 1:4-5)

CHAPTER FOUR
FREEDOM!

Dedicated to my parents, Curtis and Sarah

For the Lord is the Spirit, and wherever the Spirit of the Lord is, there is freedom.
— 2 Corinthians 3:16-18

As I wrote this, it was the day after Thanksgiving. We spent the holiday in Warren, Arkansas with Phil's side of the family. It was a cold, dreary day; much like a winter day in South Arkansas though it wasn't technically winter yet. We decided to take Tiger with us. Tiger Wayne was Olivia's little cat my mother had been keeping at her house. Phil is highly allergic to cats, so the only reason Olivia even had a cat was because my mother (affectionately known as "Gran") had offered her house as an option for a short period of time until he got big enough to either live outside or live in the barn located behind Phil's parents' house.

On this particular day, we decided to try Papaw's barn, or, at least, Phil and I decided. Olivia really wasn't up for it. I think if the weather had been better it would have been easier, but Tiger had to ride in the bed of the truck in a carrier that had become a little too small for him for an hour through wind, cold, and rain. He was fine, of course, and was carefully secured up next to the cab, but it set the tone for a hard day, not so much for Tiger, but for our sweet Olivia.

To make things more complicated, Papaw has a female cat named Stripes who rules the barn as if it belongs to her. Besides Stripes, only Kit (Papaw's horse) has "rights" to the barn. That was, until today, when Stripes' rights were challenged by a new tabby cat named Tiger, who was scared but curious, and big enough to try holding his own under less supervision than what was familiar or comfortable for him or, for that matter, anyone else.

At first, Olivia left Tiger in his carrier and placed him in his new environment so that he could get used to things slowly and safely. After a couple of hours, I suggested she and her daddy go let him out to stretch his legs and maybe see if he would eat something. They did, and, as nature would have it, Stripes took the opportunity to demonstrate her authority, and a few hairballs flew. Though Tiger did well, Olivia did not.

My usually slow-spoken, dreamy, gentle girl expressed her emphatic dislike of the whole thing through tears and a stream of words that came easily and forcefully. She was scared. She was sad. And, she wasn't ready to let Tiger go!

We took one of her shirts to the barn so Tiger would have a familiar smell to snuggle up to, and somehow I found the words to comfort her. We ended up going to get a vanilla Coke at Sonic. Olivia cleverly seized the opportunity to get me to buy her a large size, which I had never bought for her before. I didn't care though. Just seeing her eyes twinkle with that beautiful smile on her face was all I wanted, even if it did take a big vanilla Coke to get it.

Everyone stayed overnight except for me because there really wasn't room for all of us to sleep unless we chose the floor, which everyone did but me. As I drove home, my heart was full of prayers for Olivia and for Tiger. Because he means so much to her, I prayed for his safety and well-being. After all, though I cared for the cat, it was really Olivia I was concerned about. Then my thoughts turned to myself and to my love for my children. What Olivia experienced today with her cat is just the beginning of a lifetime series of heartaches and pains associated with love and letting go.

I thought, *"How on earth will I ever be able to let her go?"* The pain that struck my heart just thinking about it was enough to make me want to turn up the radio and get my mind on something else.

Human nature tends to grab hold and control as a means to protect. As a parent, I completely relate and can only imagine how hard it was for my parents to allow me to make mistakes and even get hurt as I searched for knowledge and truth. I owe much of where I am today to them for their courage in allowing me the freedom to search for answers to my many questions at a vulnerable time in my life.

I know now I was covered in prayer and that their faith in God far exceeded any worldly persuasion, for the One who was in them was greater than the one in the world (1 John 4:4). They knew that and trusted God with my life, but regardless of how you look at it, freedom is risky business.

American Feet

> "You have such soft feet!" I exclaimed.
> "I have flat feet." replied Sam.
> "Well, if you keep wearing your arches in your shoes, you'll have feet like mine," I said.
> "No!" Sam cried, "I don't want American feet!"

As an American (with American feet), I am grateful to our nation's founders for their long-sighted wisdom in establishing certain rights in the first amendments of our constitution. The first one contains the fundamental right of freedom of religion. No one can tell me or anyone else what to believe, where to assemble in that belief, or what we can say about it. That's separation of church and state in a nutshell. It's the freedom upon which America was founded. It was a risk and went beyond human nature to control things.

It's interesting to me how some people think that because one has deep faith in God that he or she doesn't believe in the separation of church and state, or even that they belong to one political party over the next. We are so quick to put labels on ourselves and on others, placing everyone in a category. We do it according to social, economic, or political status. We do it according to philosophy or education. We do it according to religion even within the same faith. We draw lines to protect what we think needs protecting and, in turn, alienate others which disarms the strength that can be found in unity *and* diversities that are God-given. It's that control thing. And it's a reality.

There's something else that is a reality and I believe stronger and more powerful than any human thought, desire, word, or action. It's the power of the fundamental freedom this country and Christianity itself are based upon — the freedom to choose by our own will. Just as no one can tell me where or how to live, there is nothing anyone can say or do that will make me believe in one religion over another, and, if it is dictated to me as a requirement for acceptance then I will only resent it and certainly never own it. My parents understood that only the Spirit of God can speak to my spirit and help me understand what is larger than my understanding. Only God can be

God, and the knowledge of that truth led to my faith today (1 Corinthians 2:10-12).

> Whenever they are attending to the Enemy Himself we are defeated, but there are ways of preventing them from doing so. The simplest is to turn their gaze away from Him towards themselves. Keep them watching their own minds and trying to produce feelings there by the action of their own wills…[1]

Out of selfish pride and ambition, Satan chose to rebel against God's authority, taking with him many other angels who also out of their own free will chose to turn against God (Isaiah 14:12-14, Revelation 12:4). This heavenly rebellion began a spiritual battle that is more real and more dangerous than anything we can see, touch, or even imagine (Ephesians 6:12).

Human beings are special creations because God placed a part of Himself within us — His breath, and His breath gave us life (Genesis 2:7). Free-thinking is an innate ability of life made in the image of God, and people are the only living things on earth that possess this quality.

The first man and woman had no wants because they had God Himself — everyday they walked with Him. He provided for them. They had nothing to fear, no insecurities, no concerns, no pain or grief or hardship. He gave them everything, and yet after listening to Satan, the Deceiver, Eve "…was convinced. She saw that the tree was beautiful and its fruit looked delicious, and she wanted the wisdom it would give her. So she took some of the fruit and ate it. Then she gave some to her husband, who was with her, and he ate it, too" (Genesis 3:6).

Out of their own free wills, Adam and Eve chose to listen to the lies (the counterfeit truths) of Satan and disobey God, who was Truth (Genesis 3:1-7). The moment this happened, what the deceitful serpent told them came true. Their eyes were opened and they became like God knowing both good and evil (Genesis 3:4). It was a truth that was twisted to attract mankind away from God by the choice of their free will, and that is the pattern of deceit this angel of evil continues today. He uses truths, things that are divinely beautiful and good and disguises them just enough to lure us away from the safety found only in the Creator of the Universe. Creation is not meant to be separated from the Creator, but that's exactly what happened when these two people exercised their freedom to choose.

Adam and Eve became aware of themselves (Genesis 3:7). That is the key. Being aware of ourselves is the root of the sinful nature that entered the human race with the first man and woman and has been passed down from that point on to generation after generation. Before we can understand anything else about ourselves or about the One who created us and saved us and guides us, we have to accept this first.

There is a part of all of us that would rather serve ourselves than serve God; that would rather do what we want to do than to do what God or anyone else for that matter wants us to do. That nature separates us from God, but He knows we cannot help it. He does not condemn us for the separation even though we *are* condemned *because* of the separation and because of the behaviors that result from it and continue to widen the gap.

We are all made in the image of God and because of that, we possess the most complex organism in the universe — the brain — that enables us to think, to learn, and to communicate. This is a marvelous freedom that was given to us by a Living God who Himself is Intelligence, Wisdom, Mercy, and Love. That is why religion and science can never be separated; they are both a part of who we are as creations in His image.

We have the ability to care for others, to recognize the difference between what is right and wrong, and to do good things. However, any behavior that is contrary to the righteousness and character of God is sin — an offense or fault according to His standard. Because we are also born with a sinful nature, we have the tendency to behave in ways that satisfy our own desires over God's desires. That in itself makes us sinners, every one of us, like it or not.

Because one woman's and one man's ambition to acquire something they thought would benefit them was greater than their desire to follow and trust the direction of the One who loved them, we are *all* separated from God by a deep spiritual chasm that we cannot cross on our own.

We think our lives are our own, but the sinful nature of our hearts constantly deceives us (Psalm 19:12). Satan is the father of lies (John 8:44). He has a plan for us and for our children, and it is the same as his plan for Adam and Eve — to persuade us to believe counterfeit truths that cause us to follow our own ambitions and invest in layers and layers of things that will ultimately hide our real identities, and separate us from God, as well as, steal the joys our Father wants to embellish upon our lives (2 Corinthians 11:3-5; 1 John 2:15-17).

Snowflakes and Fire

I can't remember not loving God. He has just always been there. As a young girl, I talked to Him all of the time especially about snow and Hell — I always wanted it to snow and I was very afraid of Hell. I didn't want anyone I loved to ever go there, so I would always end my prayers with, "and please take us all to heaven to live with you forever!"

Church was a part of my life. I went to church like I went to school. My church family was an extended part of my network of support, and I can still see the smiles and faces of so many who lovingly took care of me, who shared their lives and the stories in the Bible, and who taught me to pray. As I grew, I was active in the youth group and the music ministry. Both provided social outlets and were great fun. The music ministry in particular was an avenue that cultivated my musical abilities in addition to school. The atmosphere and the lyrics were different, but the challenge was the same.

I was baptized in grade school, but it didn't mean anything. It was a motion I went through because everyone else was doing it, and it seemed like a good thing to do. Later, during a summer youth trip, I rededicated my life. My understanding was deeper, but the motivation behind my action was still emotional. For the life of me, I can't remember being aware of the life of the Lord, Jesus Christ in any of it.

What I experienced was real and heartfelt, but the soil of my heart was shallow. I didn't own my faith. It was just a way of life. The stories of the Bible including those about Jesus were simply stories — ones I accepted as true but did not see how they applied to my life in the present day, and by the end of high school, the weeds (attractions) of the world were growing faster than the seeds of truth.

As a result, I didn't give much thought to who I was. I didn't recognize the integrity of my parents or the importance of the principles they lived by, nor did I understand the gift of their devotion to God, to each other, or to me and my sisters. I didn't see how very blessed I was and certainly didn't see any purpose in it outside of myself. I was just who I was. My identity was in who my family was (particularly at that time my father), my address, my car, my friends, my abilities, my education, my profession, my own dreams and ambitions, and even my faith in God and local church. It wasn't until I was 25 years old that I began to sense there was something I was missing and sought direction from God through prayer.

I was living in Memphis at the time and sharing a two bedroom condo in Mid-Town just off Central Avenue with a friend and former fellow graduate student. Our gated community was located right beside a railroad, directly under a flight pattern of the Memphis International Airport, and at the intersection of a busy avenue. While lying in bed and watching the headlights from cars going by my window one evening, I remember praying to God for direction for my life...*really praying* and asking Him to show me who He is and to use me for a purpose greater than myself.

I had no idea what I was asking. How often we pray for things we are not yet ready to receive and then wonder why God has not given us what we asked for when He is doing exactly that by preparing us for that which we asked!

> To say that prayer changes things is not as close to the truth as saying prayer changes me and then I change things. God has established things so that prayer, on the basis of redemption, changes the way a person looks at things. Prayer is not a matter of changing things externally but one of working miracles in a person's inner nature.[2]

It wasn't long after this that my grandfather was diagnosed with pancreatic cancer. We were told he would live only another five months at the most, and true to the statement, he died five months later. During the five months he was ill, I came home every weekend except two. Being self-employed, I only worked four days a week (leaving lots of time to play), so I left on Friday mornings and came back on Sunday afternoons. The drive from Memphis to El Dorado was almost a flat four hours, so it wasn't much of a problem.

Being home on Sunday mornings, I started attending my hometown church on a regular basis. There was a particular sermon when I remember being aware that God was leading me back to El Dorado. I don't recall anything except the butterflies in my stomach when I heard the phrase from Luke 12:34, "Wherever your treasure is, there the desires of your heart will also be."

I can still see the pastor (who later became a good friend) standing at the pulpit with the morning sun shining through the tall stained glass windows in the background. My heart was in El Dorado with my family, with my church family, with my granddaddy who was lying in a local hospital bed just a few blocks away from where I sat, and with my grandmother who was there with him. I remember thinking and trying to justify that, *"Surely my heart and my treasure can be in two different places!"*

I was very happy where I was, *very happy*, and had no intentions of moving back to my small hometown in Arkansas. Besides, I knew it would only deter me from accomplishing my long-term ambitions. I had a clear, calculated plan, and, as much as I loved my family and wanted more in life, it did not include relocating back to Arkansas.

I had to pull over on the way back to Memphis that afternoon because I was crying so hard. I was full of emotions I couldn't really distinguish but think I was mainly just sad…sad that my life was changing. My granddaddy was leaving me, and in my heart I knew my place of residence was getting ready to change. I had heard from God, and I *did not* want to do what He was asking me to do. It was the first of what would turn out to be many cross-roads, and I was very much afraid. Everything in me cried, *"No!"* My whole being, except for this small voice deep within that I had never heard before.

Looking back, I can see that God had guided me within the context of circumstances that He had allowed and placed me in a position where my mind could process His direction, and my heart was soft enough to receive it because of the grief I was experiencing through my granddaddy's illness. Although Jesus was referring to heavenly treasures, my point of reference then was from a worldly standpoint — a very self-centered standpoint — so that is where God's Holy Spirit met me. I was listening, and God of the universe came to me and met me where I was. The significance of that is overwhelming to me today. His love is amazing.

Within a few months, I was living in El Dorado. Though I did not want to be obedient, and was quite mad about the move, I had come to an intellectual conclusion in college that God did exist, and my fear of what would happen if I didn't obey His directions concerned me more than anything else.

That decision changed the direction of my life forever and marked the beginning of a series of events that eventually brought me face-to-face with my Savior and my poverty.

It was a life-saving decision that marked the beginning of what I call my "unmasking." Like an onion, I had surrounded myself unknowingly with layers and layers of things that made me feel good and confident, things that to me and to the world defined success, and mostly with things that created an image I wanted others to see. Somehow, God's voice had penetrated those layers and one by one began to slice them away.

> For the Word of God is alive and powerful. It is sharper than the sharpest two-edged sword, cutting between soul and spirit,

between joint and marrow. It exposes our innermost thoughts and desires. Nothing in all creation is hidden from God. Everything is naked and exposed before His eyes, and He is the One to whom we are accountable. (Hebrews 4:12-13)

The details don't really matter because we are all different, and God deals with us in the details of our lives on an individual basis, but the bottom line does matter because it is the same no matter who we are.

Today's world teaches that if everything looks okay on the outside, then it must be okay on the inside. Our confidence grows with layer upon layer of things that give us a false sense of security. How we look, what we have, where we live, what we do, and who we know are major factors that influence the way we see ourselves and the way we see others. The more resources we have, the more self-reliant we become, and the more we tend to pile on the layers, making it harder to peel them off.

Because we have this deep need to know who we are and what our purpose in life is, we are driven to label ourselves and each other when we look for these things outside of God. We learn to wear a mask that says "I'm okay. I have it together and I'm confident" even when we're not. We compare ourselves to a standard we set that leads to judgment, criticism, and false securities. We even find ourselves vehemently defending our positions, calling them rights and liberties, when many times our behaviors are learned and even steeped in traditional beliefs that may not be true.

Most of us are fixated on ourselves thinking too highly or too lowly but either way, equally as prideful. We are complicated and we carry burdens we were never meant to carry because we own what we only possess, and we tend to take possession of things that are only God's to handle.

> It is not true to say that God wants to teach us something in our trials. Through every cloud He brings our way, He wants us to unlearn something. His purpose in using the cloud is to simplify our beliefs until our relationship with Him is exactly like that of a child — a relationship simply between God and our own souls...[3]

Our spiritual state is the lens from which we see the world. If we "own" what we see, then we do not have an accurate understanding of God, of ourselves, or each other. However, if we are "poor" and have the spiritual understanding that we do not "own" a thing except our faith then poverty is the lens that enables us to see the Kingdom of Heaven in everything, in ourselves, in our possessions, in our circumstances, and in others. When we are (spiritually) poor, we are (spiritually) rich and, therefore, like Paul we can find contentment in little or in much (Philippians 4:11-12). We can offer our lives as a sacrifice of thanksgiving to Him out of love, not obligation, or guilt, or shame, or fear.

When Jesus said we must give up everything we own to follow Him (Luke 14:33), I don't think He was talking about physical poverty. I believe He was talking about spiritual poverty; the intellectual understanding that *we are nothing and have nothing without Christ.* The thing is, many times we say that we know this, but our actions prove otherwise. Giving up what we own is the acid test — especially for those of us who have much like the rich young ruler in Matthew (19:16-30). We simply value so many things more than we value our relationship with Christ, and because of that, we are not free. We are enslaved, and we don't even realize it.

My life was so about me, the soil of my heart was too hard for the seeds of truth I had heard throughout my childhood to take root and grow (Matthew 13:5-6, 20-21). It took five years for God to even begin answering my prayer to know Him and to be used for a purpose greater than myself because there was so much ground to cultivate in my heart and in my thinking, so many weeds to pull out, and so many seeds that needed nurturing (Matthew 13:7, 22).

As I look back now, I am so thankful for the seeds of truth that had been planted in my life when I was young and for the prayer that had watered and protected them while they lay dormant waiting for the right season to grow.

I used to think life was just a journey that was full of the normal ups and downs, good times and bad times we all go through with the destination being happiness; happiness that was rooted in reputation, possessions, relationships, opportunities, and independence. For me that equated to a life based on traditional and conservative values; a life that was well balanced, controlled, and non-controversial with a nice family, nice home, nice bank account, nice car, nice clothes, and nice personality laced with work, vacations, church, and community.

There is absolutely nothing wrong with this picture. It's a great picture — an American dream, but if we are living the dream without understanding reality, we are only going through the motions detached from our source. Eventually, it will play out, and we will either wake up disillusioned and filled with regrets or the dream will become a living nightmare from which there is no awakening.

> I am the way, the truth, and the life. No one can come to the Father except through Me. (John 14:6)

Truth sets us free (Galatians 5:1). Only in the face of Christ do we see who we really are, and that all-important life lesson can only be taught by the LORD Himself. Only He can teach us without wounding us. Only He can set us free from the layers encrusted upon our lives that hide our true selves and suffocate His identity in us. Only He can set us free because only He is Truth, and because of that we are free to release all of the burdens we hold so tightly and hold loosely all of the things we so dearly love.

In a very real way, we are free to be poor and, for many, that may equate to weakness, but when we walk in the light as He is in the light, we are free to be who we are and to let the Holy Spirit be our teacher and Christ be our judge. We are free to take hold of the hand that so longs to lead us and to trust Him more than ourselves or man.

I have learned that the greatest power I have lies within the very freedom God has given me and is available to all who will receive; the freedom to choose what is right, the freedom to discern what is true, and the freedom to embrace what is outside myself and higher than what I can reduce to something cognizant.

When we sincerely and without selfish motivation reach out to God and ask Him to reveal Himself to us, to fill us, and to use us for the sole purpose that He may be known and enjoyed, we are praying on His behalf. We are putting Him before ourselves, and we can be certain that He will answer because this is the will of God (1 Corinthians 10:31; Psalm 73:25-26) and the chief end of man.[4]

God's plan is to redeem you, to take back what belongs to Him and give you abundant life now and eternal life in the future — both found in Him. He left His perfect, heavenly home and became human so that as a human (and at the same time fully God), He could take upon Himself all the sin of the world — that means every sin of every person who has ever lived, who is living, and who will live in the future — sacrifice His life by dying on a cross, and overcome death. By this, He became the supernatural, divine path that leads to God — to *Life* (John 11:25-26; Philippians 2:6-11)! There is no other way to God because there can be no other way to Him except through Him as Jesus Christ (Psalm 18:31). Anything else is a counterfeit truth and complete lie.

It's very simple. If we put our trust in anything outside of Him and His ways, we will fall prey to Satan's strategies, and we will lose the very lives we so long to save (Luke 9:24).

Just like the mysteries of creation do not exist outside of the Creator, there is no life apart from the Living God. He is Life. Apart from Him there is nothing but death which explains the voids in our lives that are never filled by counterfeit treasures.

Because of Him and His unfailing love, I am free to be holy. I am free to turn from my sin and any traditional belief or practice that keeps me from expressing holiness. I am free to recognize the value of life in *every* face because each face mirrors my God, even though I understand each heart does not mirror His love. I am free to meet people where they are and to love them regardless of where that is because that is exactly what He did for me.

No matter who you are or what you've done; no matter what you have or what you lack; no matter how full or how empty your life seems to be, God through Jesus Christ came to set you free. He is the love you are looking for.

> But don't just listen to God's word. You must do what it says. Otherwise, you are only fooling yourselves. For if you listen to the word and don't obey, it is like glancing at your face in a mirror. You see yourself, walk away, and forget what you look like. But if you look carefully into the perfect law that sets you free, and if you do what it says and don't forget what you heard, then God will bless you for doing it. (James 1:22-25)

Notes

[1] C.S. Lewis, *The Screwtape Letters* (New York: Harper Collins, 1996), 16.

[2] Oswald Chambers, *My Utmost for His Highest* (Oswald Chambers Publication Association, Ltd. 1992), August 28.

[3] Chambers, *My Utmost for His Highest*, July 29.

[4] Westminster Assembly, *Westminster Catechism* (London, 1646), Question 1, Answer 1.

CHAPTER FIVE

Dying with Grace

Dedicated to all who are running The Great Race,
In memory of those who have finished, and in honor of the ones who love them.

With special memory of Laurie who is forever 41

*...And let us run with endurance the race
God has set before us.
— Hebrews 12:1*

Being confident in my good health, I was taken off guard when I received the diagnosis of breast cancer. I hadn't been feeling well for several weeks and had started waking up as tired as I was the night before. My clothes seemed to be fitting a little looser, but my appetite was strangely increasing.

I actually took a pregnancy test thinking (and getting a little excited about the possibility) that I just might be pregnant, but it was negative. I took it again a week later because I just *knew* I was pregnant; I had to be! My body was not the same and I was so tired. What else could it be, I thought? It hadn't been more than two months since I had been approved for the highest level and lowest rate of life insurance because my health was so good. Again, negative.

It occurred to me at that point that some blood work was needed, and I was overdue any way for a yearly visit with my doctor, so I made an appointment to see my physician. In the meantime, I noticed a swollen place under my arm. Although the logical opinion of my physician was to take an antibiotic and recheck in a month, my gut told me to get a second opinion.

So, I did, and an ultrasound was ordered. Within a week, I was referred to a breast cancer specialist.

I remember standing on the front porch with Phil on a beautiful day when we got the phone call with the news. I didn't know much about cancer, so my first thought was about death. The thought of going home — my true *home*, though it seemed premature, was a little exciting. The relief and safety and complete joy of being where I belong and long to be was appealing, and a part of me was ready to go, but before I could even exhale from that thought, my heart felt a great pain in the realization of what I would be leaving behind.

I remember looking into the faces of my three children, then ages 5, 6, and 10, as I told them individually I had this thing called cancer and was going to be seeing the doctor a lot. Sam was first, then John, and then Olivia. I guess it was easier for me in that order and helped me build confidence as the conversations grew more serious with each one.

Sam, in his usual quiet way, internalized it and didn't ask questions. He just said "okay," and kept playing with his cars and trains. Of course, he was only five years old and had been home with us two years. He didn't have the vocabulary or knowledge that Olivia and John both had. This was a good thing for him and allowed him to learn at a pace he could absorb and process as things evolved.

Olivia and John, on the other hand, both knew that cancer was more serious than a cold or the flu. John was sitting up in our bed watching television when I sat beside him and, as if announcing he had more homework to do, I told him the news. It was the only way I knew to keep from creating any more fear than I knew he would already feel, and to keep my own emotions in check.

I asked him if he had ever heard of the word "cancer." His eyes widened and locked onto mine as he said in his typical, no nonsense way, "Yeah, kids die from it. Are you going to die?"

I should have known John would get to the heart of the matter. The big, gray elephant that we try to avoid or pretend is not even in the room just doesn't have a chance around him. John immediately sits the elephant in your lap and forces you to deal with it! "Well, I'm going to die someday, and so will you — we all will, but just because I have cancer, it doesn't mean I'm going to die."

My conversation with Olivia was the same, but a little more intense; the same big question but many more little ones. She was sitting up in bed too. Funny, how images like that remain engraved in our minds like photographs.

I felt better after talking to them. Their candor gave me strength to just face the facts, and their sweet little faces gave me a determination to pray for them as I never had before.

The type of cancer I had was very aggressive, HER2 — driven, and "inflammatory;" the type that explodes out from the site of origin where it then begins to move through the body quickly. It's rare — making up only about 3% of all breast cancers. By the time it was found, I had three tumors and many affected lymph nodes with the likelihood the cancer cells had invaded my bloodstream and begun to settle into my organs.

There are a host of things that go through one's mind when faced with death. Like countless others, I found myself in the throes of a battle I did not choose, and one that was encroaching quickly, threatening to overtake my life and what I loved; requiring a fight for survival. Though there is a nationwide fight for a cure, for me, it was a very personal one. It was a fight to trust others with my care and discern the decisions that had to be made; a fight to endure difficult days of poor health and a negative attitude that frequently went along with it; a fight to retain courage and not sink in the despair of fear; a fight not to blame myself and wonder what I did wrong. Some days, it was just a fight to hope and not give up, and a fight to remember what I knew.

When you have nothing else, you have what you know.
— Dr. Lyndell P. Worthen, Jr.[1]

For almost two decades, I had been trying to figure out what exactly it was that I knew. Little by little, I had learned that what I believe in my heart and mind to be true provides a foundation upon which every decision is built and a filter through which all thoughts are processed. These beliefs mold my attitude and my response to circumstances that greatly affect the way I perceive, respond, and interact. They are the things I live by, whether consciously or not, that determine the course of my life in every aspect, both professionally and personally, that cannot without futility be separated (though I had given much effort to do so).

When we took our family pictures just prior to my first round of chemotherapy, my thoughts of what was to come centered on physical changes — my presence with my family, what I would look like when I lost my hair, how I would feel, how it would affect my work, what I would do if this happened or if that happened. I wasn't aware of the deep transformation this thing called cancer was about to bring to my life; what it would do to my heart through the power of my thoughts, and how it would pierce my soul. The wife and mother in the family pictures that now adorn our home, with long, dark hair and body intact, has certainly changed in many ways — the physical changes being the very least.

When I think back to those days, the difficulties have thankfully faded, but there were treasures found along the way that I will cherish and remember for the rest of my life. The amazing taste and smell of coffee exactly eight days after the chemo wore off, the smell of fresh cut flowers from the garden and the softness of rose petals against my skin, the laughter and smile of my sweet friend, Sandra, when she brought our weekly loaf of homemade bread (whose face now lights up the heavens), the taste of watermelon with salt (one of the only things I could eat or enjoy for a while), the cool breeze through opened windows, the warm voices on the phone, the hands that wrote the notes, the hearts that interceded for me, the steadiness of my husband, the courage of my kids, my mom in the kitchen, the concern of my loved ones, the power of thanksgiving, the comfort of home, the clarity of importance, and the precious gift of time.

I have never experienced such love or seen people in the way I saw them during that time in my life. From my family and friends to my coworkers and neighbors to my doctors and nurses, the lab technicians and the patients; those who no longer grace this earth for losing their own battles and the loved ones they left behind to the many more who still fight today, they are the treasures I hold near my heart. Their lives are the footholds that enabled me to climb to a greater height, and their souls are what I see as I look down into the valley where we all live day by day.

Facing death brought me life — true life, in all of its fullness, that begins and ends with the knowledge and understanding of who I am, who I am not, and a purpose that the eye cannot see without the heart, and perhaps the heart cannot understand without suffering.

Hinds Feet on High Places by Hannah Hurnard is a beautiful allegory based on the Song of Solomon, Psalm 18:33 and Habakkuk 3:19 that has become one of my most treasured readings. It is the story of how little Much-Afraid, who lived in the Valley of Humiliation, followed the Shepherd to the High Places with Sorrow and Suffering as her companions. The quote just after the title page sums up the book best:

> There are no obstacles which our Savior's love cannot overcome. The High Places of victory and union with Christ can be reached by learning to accept, day by day, the actual conditions

and tests permitted by God, by laying down of our own will and accepting His. The lessons of accepting and triumphing over evil, of becoming acquainted with grief, and pain, and of finding them transformed into something incomparably precious; these are the lessons of the allegory in this book.[2]

We are connected by the goodness and love that comes from the image of God in each of us as well as the effects of a fallen world in and upon our lives. Now I know what it is like to be limited physically and mentally as well; to grieve over the loss of my good health, and to surrender to what I have no control over. Cancer has heightened my perspective of life for so many who suffer from disabling situations, from illness and disease, and especially for those who are brokenhearted, who are vulnerable and "crippled" without the support of someone who loves and believes in them. For that, this illness has been a gift and has deepened my faith in God and love for others; a joy from suffering I wouldn't change for the world.

It was late in December, 2010, after almost two years of treatment, when I finally told my doctor that my back was hurting around my shoulder blade. It wasn't a normal hurt, and I knew there was a real possibility the cancer had spread. He ordered an immediate bone scan, and I could see the concern on his face. The scan takes 20-30 minutes — long enough to take a nap, but there was no sleeping on this particular afternoon. I was fully awake and strangely calm.

As I lay there, I finally realized that nothing has permission from God to defeat us. He has overcome the world (John 16:33). That means that even in death — if that is what He allows despite our love for Him — we are not defeated. We are delivered, and He is responsible for the consequences — being fully able to do immeasurably more than we could imagine or ask (Ephesians 3:20).

Though I did not understand why God was allowing me to go through the illness of cancer, I had learned I could trust Him. If there was one thing he had taught me over the years, it was the undeniable truth that my life was not my own. It belonged completely to Him to do whatever He desired, and his desire was always good. He knew how much I loved Him. He knew how much I wanted His absolute best and fullness for my children. He knew I was weak and sinful and scared. He knew I trusted Him. And, I knew He could be trusted.

If I could just embrace the sufficiency of His grace and be obedient in the moment, I would learn and be strengthened no matter how the scan turned out. I couldn't make the difference I wanted to make in the lives of my children or in anyone else's life by holding on to my own. He was my expectation, and I had to let go.

So, while lying as still as possible in that small, dark room while the bone scan ran over my body, I died that afternoon. I was 41.

> There is a connection between the strange providential circumstances allowed by God and what we know of Him, and we have to learn to interpret the mysteries of life in the light of our knowledge of God. Until we can come face to face with the deepest, darkest fact of life without damaging our view of God's character, we do not yet know Him.[3]

I think Job's life is one of the greatest illustrations of God's promise of faithfulness in our poverty. For a while, Job became so isolated in the devastation of his circumstances that he lost all hope and wanted to die. It's easy to give up in the center of trouble, but God reminded Job who *He* was, and by remaining true to that great reality, Job received his life.

It is no different for you or me. Job's life is proof that God is waiting to remind us who He is no matter what devastating circumstances we find ourselves facing. He doesn't change; His love and faithfulness endure forever (Psalm 119:88-90). It is *our* faith that fails, our faith *in Him* not in the things we know He can do or hope will happen. Job saw God in every circumstance and, therefore, trusted Him beyond logic. His view of God's character did not change even in his darkest hour, and that is the lesson I have learned from his life.

The Real War

"It is much easier to die than to lay down your life day in and day out with the sense of the high calling of God."[4] The pain in my shoulder blade and spine never returned. I suppose it could've been my imagination, and, then again, it could be that God healed me on that table — I don't know. It doesn't matter. Regardless of my physical health, something much deeper happened to me. Something I can't touch or even explain, but I can tell you the words of Jeremiah became my own, "I know, LORD, that our lives are not our own. We are not able to plan our own course. So correct me, LORD, but please be gentle" (Jeremiah 10:23-24).

The battle of cancer was over, but the fight was just beginning. I was excited but concerned because I knew I wasn't strong enough to do what would be required. Things had changed. The journey during the last ten years had depleted many things including my stamina, and I was tempted to just stay in the boat to weather the storms.

I think it would have been okay for me to do that — to stay in the boat, but I was keenly aware that if God was asking me for something more then there was a reason for it, and I found myself in a different kind of fight; a fight within my own will. If I was going to get out of the boat, then I was going to have to get rid of it so that I couldn't get back in. Otherwise, I knew I would retreat.

It reminded me of a story I read many years earlier about a great warrior who faced a situation that required him to do something drastic in order to win in a very difficult battle. He and his soldiers were getting ready to engage in a fight against an army that was much larger and stronger than theirs. The great warrior knew the success of the battle would be determined by the attitudes of his soldiers. Their success would come only from a burning passion to win. So, he loaded his men on boats and sailed to the country of their enemies. Once they unloaded, he had the ships burned. They would either win or they would die; there would be no retreat.[5]

Out physical situations may not be life or death as in the story above, but, spiritually, that is exactly what they are. The boat may represent something different to each of us, but for all of us, that something may have to be released in order to keep us focused and moving toward the finish line.

> Above all else, guard your heart, for it is the wellspring of life.
> (Proverbs 4:23 NIV)

For reasons I do not understand and never will on this side of life, God chose to continue the work of reconciling the world back to Him through Christ *in us*. Because He has chosen us as vessels through which to work, He must have full access to our lives through our minds and our hearts. Otherwise, it would be a task that we ourselves could accomplish, but, of course, that would be a position of complete and utter arrogance. It is only a battle that He can win through His life in us which is why the only thing He requires of us is to act justly, love mercy, and walk humbly with Him (Micah 6:8 NIV).

Because of the gift of free will, however, the state of the soil of our hearts is largely up to us. He can work through us regardless and does, but the fullness of His life and the life He longs to give is hindered if we're not surrendered to Him. He always has more to teach, more to reveal, and more to give. How much we are able to learn and unlearn, to envision and receive depends on our willingness to submit. Unless we give Him access, the soil will never be ready to produce a full harvest.

The fight to yield to God's authority is, for me, by far the toughest battle yet. I'm not mad about it like I was in my twenties because my motivation now is love, not fear. But, it is hard. It's a daily challenge, and I'm probably misunderstood more than I realize, but it doesn't matter. Those things fade in comparison to God Himself.

Though I am tired, I am at peace; a little shaken but in some ways stronger than ever, for, I know that in life or in death, true hope and healing are possible only through the love and power of Christ. We can be sure His desires are good and can be trusted even when it appears another way.

> The LORD cares deeply when His loved ones die. O Lord, I am your servant; yes, I am your servant, born into your household; you have freed me from my chains. I will offer you a sacrifice of thanksgiving and call on the name of the LORD. I will fulfill my vows to the LORD in the presence of all His people — in the house of the LORD in the heart of Jerusalem. Praise the LORD!" (Psalm 116:15-19)

Notes

[1] Dr.Lyndell P. Worthen, Jr., Pastor, First Baptist Church, El Dorado, Arkansas, 1996-2011.

[2] Hannah Hurnard, *Hinds' Feet on High Places* (Uhrichsville: Barbour Publishing, Inc.) page after title page.

[3] Oswald Chambers, *My Utmost for His Highest* (Oswald Chambers Publication Association, Ltd. 1992), July 29.

[4] Ibid, June 16.

[5] Napoleon Hill, *Think and Grow Rich* (New York: Jeremy P. Tarcher/Penguin Group, 2008), 24-25.

CHAPTER SIX

Courage of Presence

Dedicated to my forever family in Christ Jesus —
those in Heaven, those on Earth and those who
have not yet been "born."
In honor of my local family of faith and my Cooperative Baptist
Fellowship friends

*…only in returning to me and resting in me will you be saved. In
quietness and confidence is your strength…*
— Isaiah 30:15

I have been exposed to and involved in the Christian faith all of my life but have walked with Jesus only the last 15 years.

I have learned that it takes courage to walk with Jesus. Dying is certainly gain because the alternative that Paul spoke of ("to live is Christ") is just plain hard on this side of Heaven (Philippians 1:21)!

When I examine my life and all that I have experienced, my heart grieves over many things. I was so stupid. So blind. So prideful and self-righteous. And yet I can see God's mercy and love and guidance through every moment. His fingerprints are all over my life.

I guess I grew up thinking that the Church was something different than the rest of my life. It was a part of my life — the special part — that was much like the cherry on top of a lot of other good things. Missions, talking about God, prayer, Bible study, all of that took place at church or with "the church." It did not take place outside of Sundays or Wednesday nights. I really believe that because I had this wrong idea about the church, I easily fell away from it. It simply didn't hold up under the pressures of the world as I got older because the world was so much more attractive.

That is hard to say, but it is the truth, and I have to say it. It is one of the main reasons I am writing this book and also one of the primary reasons I do not want to write it. It's embarrassing. With the kind of examples and support I had through my family and church family, I should have known better... right?

It reminds me of Eve, and gives me compassion for her. Of ALL people, she should have known better. Giving in to what she wanted for an immediate and short term satisfaction cost her and the rest of creation more than she could have ever imagined. I don't think she could have fathomed the gravity of her decision.

Though first I had to intellectually work through accepting the knowledge of who Jesus was and is before my heart could respond to Him, the condition of my heart also had to be cultivated. That is something only God can do, and I think sometimes we forget that.

No matter how many layers I have packed on to make myself feel important or secure, God, my Father, sees my soul at the core of it all and lovingly reaches out and prunes me. He does the same for all of us who are growing in the soil of faith, and He knows exactly what branches to cut, what weeds to pull out, and what fruit (yes, even *good fruit*) to remove, so that our souls have the opportunity to thrive and reach their greatest potential.

In an ideal world, there would be no disruption or alternative pattern in what God created to be holy. However, the fact is we don't live in an ideal world. We live in a fallen world; a world full of sin, full of suffering and full of pain. There are so many things we don't understand, so many circumstances out of our control and so many times we knowingly and unknowingly hurt ourselves and each other by the choices we make. We live in a world full of wounded people — a world that Almighty, Most Holy God through Jesus Christ died to redeem; a world that has changed dramatically over time that only His life can redeem today.

If I am who I say I am as a follower of Christ, then there is a different standard for me that does not apply to those who do not know Him. However, those who share this understanding only share this understanding. The conditions of our hearts, the layers, the wounds, the "working out" of our salvation we do NOT share. Like the disciples responded differently to Jesus, my response to the truth of His life is uniquely my own. It is different for each one of us, but it is the same God who leads us all for the same purpose and destination through Christ.

His resurrected life bridges the gap across the chasm that separates us from God, and that is something so wonderful I have no words to express my thanksgiving. However, the way He lived, the words He chose, the manner in which He related to others and the decisions He made are examples He set for us to follow — a work of His life up until His death that also transcends time and culture just like His work on the cross.

In order to pave the way for man to be with God (which is where our true home lies), Jesus had to fully identify with man by giving up every aspect of His deity. He couldn't break the hold of death upon our lives without becoming one of us, and in so doing, not only created a supernatural pathway for our souls to be with God, but also revealed the secret of victory in all earthly circumstances (Hebrews 2: 14-17, Romans 12: 9-21).

He chose to humble Himself and become a servant to those who were unworthy (John 13:14-15). He loved when He wasn't loved (Mark 10:21). He forgave when there was no repentance (Luke 23:34). He was merciful when it wasn't deserved (John 8:1-11), and He allowed Himself to be subject to the sin and arrogance of others without defending Himself or pushing back (Luke 23:8-11). His life was an expression that those of us who have been united with Him in faith and love are expected to follow (Galatians 3: 26-28); an expression that not only conveys we will suffer in the same ways (in addition to the consequences of our own sins) but one that gives us the courage to let it come, knowing there is nothing that can conquer us or take our joy unless we allow it (John 16:33).

By loving Him in response to His love for us and by identifying with Him the way He identified with us, we enter into a covenant and protected relationship that not only anchors our souls but secures His will on earth as in heaven. We can let go of the guilt and obligation we feel when we pressure ourselves to *make* things happen and just follow His lead every day, allowing Him to guide us through the mess in our lives and in this world that only He understands.

True freedom comes when we recognize this absolute control and authority of Jesus Christ (Galatians 5:1). It is a message with a platform uniquely its own that cannot go to the world on anyone's terms but must be given the room (the liberty) to bring others to it. It is a message that is bound *in* Christ, not in our ideas *about* Christ or a mold we want everyone to fit nicely into.

I am a sinner. No matter how hard I try to think and do what is right, I can't — not without salvation of God through Christ and the guidance of His Holy Spirit in me. There is nothing I can do for Him other than surrender to Him my life as a vessel through which He then uses to touch others. Without Him, I cannot forgive. I am not merciful. I am certainly not patient or kind and, if the truth be told, sometimes I don't want to be. Because of my free will, it is up to me how much of my heart I release to Him.

The Real Deal

I heard the president of K-LOVE, a Christian radio station, say during one of their pledge drives recently that they are a "ministry of presence," and a "ministry of being." It made me think about my friends in the Cooperative Baptist Fellowship who also strive to be the presence of Christ in the world and reminded me of the encounter that Jesus had with a Samaritan woman (John 4: 1-38). I have thought about what it must have been like for this woman many times, and I find my heart is so jealous of what she experienced.

As she visited with Jesus at the well, she was fully in His presence. There was no one else around. It was just Him and her, face-to-face. She was blessed beyond what I think any of us can imagine. Having the full attention of Jesus in person, she looked into His eyes. She heard the audible sound of His voice as He spoke directly to her. She saw His rugged hands, His dirty feet, and the shape of His face as it changed when He smiled at her. Perhaps she sensed weariness in His posture or noted something strangely familiar in His mannerisms. There is no way to know, but one thing is certain, her thinking and her life changed because of His presence.

He *knew* her. He knew everything about her, and yet He cared for her. She could tell, and it made a difference in the condition of her heart and her mind. It enabled her to hear His words and receive and believe Truth, and once she believed, she was motivated to bring others to meet Him — even those who had hurt and rejected her — because she saw that He was greater than all of the things that brought her pain, even her own sin. She knew in her heart that in Him, there was both safety and healing.

It often seems that we try to be Jesus when all we can do and all He expects of us is to be the vessels through which His life touches others, like a pipe that the Water of Life runs through. We are ambassadors of divine nature with human limitations (2 Corinthians 5:11-21). We are souls with bodies, not bodies with souls, as I have heard Kerry and Chris Shook say in a DVD based on their book, *One Month to Live: 30 Days to a No-Regrets Life*. Faithfully representing God through Christ requires a total surrender to the guidance of the Holy Spirit that enables us to truly be the presence of Christ in the world without our interference.

> "Genuine total surrender is a personal sovereign preference for Jesus Christ Himself."[1]

Only God has the privilege of knowing every heart and being totally trustworthy which is why salvation, the working out of salvation, and judgment are His responsibilities and His alone (James 4:11-12, Proverbs 15:11). It doesn't mean those who share faith in Christ should look the other way and refuse to address issues that are harmful to the fellowship and unity of the Body of Christ (Ephesians 4: 1-6). It simply means we must mirror the same kindness, the same patience, and the same self-control in all of our relationships as our Lord extends to us (Romans 2:4). And, if we cannot, then perhaps our silence can, for it is sometimes not what we say but what we do not say that speaks loudest and is most effective (James 1:19, 26; James 2:21-26).

During a Student Leadership 201 conference in Washington D.C. that I attended with Olivia and several of her high school classmates, I heard a statement that is worth repeating. Brent Crowe was speaking about some gray areas in the Christian life — issues that tend to spike controversy. Unlike the saying we have heard so often, *"Love the sinner; hate the sin,"* Brent challenged the students and those of us with them to *"Love the sinner: hate your own sin."* Such a small difference in wording causes a huge shift in perspective (James 4: 7-12; Matthew 7:1-6).

Jesus is The Word (John 1:1). His life accomplished many things we cannot fully comprehend, for although we have the Bible and we have the Holy Spirit, no one has full knowledge of objective truth (James 4:7-12; Matthew 7:1-6). We cannot discern God's will through reason alone because what we see is only partial and what we understand is limited (1 Corinthians 13:9-12). There is so much we have yet to discover about the heart and mind of God (Ephesians 3:19).

One thing we do know, however, is that Christ transforms lives — not our theology or what we think about Him. His character reaches places we don't even know are there in the human soul, and He reveals Himself to whomever, however, wherever and whenever He pleases. Though He uses others to guide us, it is He alone that longs to be our teacher (Matthew 11: 27-30). Once a person believes and accepts the "Living Water" of His life, then the Holy Spirit will help with the choices that are made over time.

That is why His yoke is light. It's not up to us. It's up to Him through us and God's Holy Spirit in us (2 Corinthians 5:19-21). As His ambassadors, we are responsible for surrendering our wills (laying down our lives for our Friend and friends) (John 15:13-15), obeying His directions, and imitating His ways to the best of our abilities so that His Life is free to touch and heal as He pleases. He is responsible for the consequences, and we can be sure that if He is in control, the results can be trusted.

> "Don't you see how wonderfully kind, tolerant, and patient God is with you? Does this mean nothing to you? Can't you see that His kindness is intended to turn you from your sin?" (Romans 2:4)

A Higher Perspective

By the end of our 18-day trip overseas to bring our son, Sam, home from the country in which he was born, Phil and I were more than ready to get home. During those days, we flew eight different times, traveled to nine different cities, and stayed over the course of the trip in hotels where people spoke little English. In each city, we were hosted by interpreters, who were native to China, bi- or multi-lingual, and dedicated to serving the needs of orphaned children. They were a blessing to us and shared their country, their culture, and their view of the world with graciousness.

We were in China during the Chinese New Year. It was the Year of the Pig (I remember because I have a picture of Sam sitting by this HUGE lighted pig in the lobby of the last hotel where we stayed in Guangzhou). We toured many places and saw many things that give China its distinction in the world. The place that brought me the most intrigue, however, was a place of worship on top of a beautiful mountain.

I watched as countless people burned incense, bowed, and appeared to pray to golden statues...one after the other. It was a beautiful day and very peaceful where we were; a place conducive for worship for sure because of all the natural beauty of creation surrounding us, but the only thing I remember is how lonely it felt. In fact, though we were surrounded by what seemed like oceans of people at times, the air of loneliness was ever present.

As we boarded the plane that would take us from China back to the United States, I was on the verge of tears. We had held things together pretty well, and definitely developed a love for China and its precious people that would continue to burn in our hearts for the rest of our lives. Because of Sam, the Chinese culture had become a part of us. We were now a multicultural family, not just a family with a multicultural child. Our hearts were so grateful for this wonderful gift, but as good as that was, *home* was calling.

I remember anxiously awaiting the first sign of land, constantly looking out the window and scanning the horizon for the United States' west coast. The words, "proud to be an American," that is familiar to many, rang through my mind like a strained chord. At that moment, those words held new meaning.

I wasn't proud to be an American, I was *thankful* to be an American. I was thankful for my home and the opportunities it afforded me and my loved ones. I was thankful for the ones who had sacrificed their lives so that we could live freely, and I was horrified by the fact that I had taken my freedom for granted while, at the same time, felt the freedom of others should be limited simply because they see life from a point of view I do not have or understand.

That realization opened a whole new dimension of thinking and gave me a perspective on life I had never seen before. I have to admit, it was startling, but I knew in my heart it was right. By trusting Him in obedience, God had placed me in a position where He was able to lift my understanding of freedom and faith *in His sovereignty* to an even greater height than I could see from the view in the plane.

> It takes God a long time to get us to stop thinking that unless everyone sees things exactly as we do, they must be wrong. That is never God's view. There is only one true liberty — the liberty of Jesus at work in our conscience enabling us to do what is right.[2]

I have always thought of a nation as being defined by the ruling authorities, the government and the law. Though there is certainly a trickle-down effect from decisions made within top leadership that impacts the life of every citizen, I have come to understand that true power lies in the people. The nation is you, and it is me. We are different and yet the same.

If you peel back the top layer of skin, we all have a similar appearance. We're made of bones and tissues and blood. We are spiritual beings in physical bodies with souls that thirst for acceptance, worth, and love. Our differences come in the unique ways God has fashioned each of us as well as in our circumstances, in the ways those circumstances influence our thinking, and in the ways our thinking drives our actions to quench this universal thirst and fill the void it creates.

We are all flawed and imperfect, needing the grace of God to cover us as we individually work out our salvation (allow God to mold and shape our character into the likeness of Christ) (Philippians 2:12). Accepting His Lordship and authority over our lives takes time. It doesn't happen overnight, especially for those who have so many layers of wounds and false securities. But it does happen as our relationship with Him grows. The depth and breadth of that depends on the individual, and in the case of others, it depends on how much we as Christ's ambassadors are willing to support them with the life of Christ in us.

Jesus never made anyone feel bad about who they were, but He always spoke the truth without contradicting His character. He was the gospel, and because of that He had an advantage over us. He knew the hearts of all the people and was able to establish credibility almost instantaneously by getting to the heart of the matter. In essence, He *was relationship*. We are not and, therefore, we have to make the effort to build relationships with others by truly sharing in their lives and walking beside them on common ground, allowing the life of Christ in us to guide us as we reach out to them.

Even the disciples who loved Christ and knew Him intimately, spending nearly every waking hour with Him over a period of many months, did not fully comprehend who He was at times or what that meant for them because their hearts were too hard (Mark 6:52). Even so, Jesus continued to love them, continued to teach them, continued to stay in the "Valley of Humiliation"[3] until God called Him home.

The plan hasn't changed. His life can continue to love, teach, and accompany each one of us through the guidance of God through His Holy Spirit. The process is different, but the results are the same.

When John was seven years old, he walked into the room where I was sitting with the most down-and-out face I had seen in a while. In his little gruff voice, he asked, "Mama, what do I want to be when I grow up?"

"Well, John," I replied with a smile, "You're only seven years old; you don't have to figure that out right now."

With my response not helping him, he further explained with increasing emotion, "Well, I had to write a story in school today about what I wanted to be and I said a policeman, but I don't want to be a policeman! I want to be a famous football player!"

"How about a doctor?" I said. "I think you'd make a great doctor."

In horror with eyes bulging, John responded, "I don't want to KILL someone!"

"John, doctors don't kill people, they help people," I corrected.

"Not always! Sometimes they kill people on ACCIDENT!"

John's heart and words showed depth of wisdom for such a little boy. Even with the best of intentions, we really do hurt people, and sadly sometimes it's no accident at all. We spend so much energy and time trying to persuade, convert, and guide people according to our way of thinking and what we believe is right that we forget to love them. And, in the process we harm or break what is already a bruised reed (Isaiah 42:3, Matthew 12:20).

No one but Christ can touch our sinful natures or heal our broken hearts (Isaiah 61:1), and yet we so often take upon ourselves the position of being moral guides[4] and set ourselves and our thinking as a principle for others that cannot be reached because of the unique paths they are on and the layers that are keeping God's word and truth from penetrating their hearts.

I am doing nothing for the Kingdom of God by pointing a finger and telling people how they should live and using myself and my God as the standard when they don't understand who God is, when they don't understand the love and reason of Christ, and when they don't see anything different or attractive in me (Colossians 4:5-6). Instead, I would only push them away and cut short any influence I might have to truly be an ambassador for Christ's Kingdom and help them see and connect to Him in some way.

We have to understand that if people are not walking in freedom or are struggling in some way (especially in America and the "Bible belt" where there are churches on every corner and preachers on television every time you flip through the stations), there are probably layers and layers of reasons for this; layers that only God through His Holy Spirit understands and can penetrate.

Jesus was God in just one man, but now that He has taken His rightful place as our heavenly High Priest, the Holy Spirit lives in each one who trusts Christ for eternal life with God. By that, we are His witnesses. Together, we have the power to do "even greater things" (John 14:12) than Jesus did because of God's Spirit in us if we will just listen to Him and allow others the right to listen too.

With the seven billion people in the world and 316 million in the U.S. alone*, there is a reason we are made differently. We think differently, we process information differently, we approach problems differently, we interpret differently, we act differently, we express ourselves differently, and so on and so on. Truth never changes, but to fully understand and express God's truths, we need each other.

Where the Rubber Meets the Road

In Luke 5:1-11, we read about Peter and his business partners, James and John. They were fishermen and they had fished all night long without catching a thing. After listening to Jesus teach, Jesus instructed him to take his boat further into deeper water and cast the nets again. Peter was reluctant but did so only because Jesus asked him to. The result was a catch so large, the nets began to tear, and he had to call for his partners to help. That was amazing, but the more amazing part is the response of these men.

> When Simon Peter realized what had happened, he fell to his knees before Jesus and said, 'Oh, Lord, please leave me — I'm too much of a sinner to be around you.' For he was awestruck by the number of fish they had caught, as were the others with him. His partners, James and John, the sons of Zebedee, were also amazed. Jesus replied to Simon, 'Don't be afraid! From now on you'll be fishing for people!' And as soon as they landed, they left everything and followed Jesus. (Luke 5:8-11)

The presence of Christ demands a response from us, and our response is an indication of whether we are for Him or against Him in that moment. When we obey what we sincerely believe He is asking of us, it opens the door for Him to reveal Himself and His power to us. When this happens, we are able to see ourselves for who we really are. Like Peter, James, and John, our hearts become pliable (or "plow"-able) and our priorities change as things become a little clearer with each step we take.

Through the Holy Spirit, God is able to transform our natural tendencies into something new (Ephesians 4:23-24). He gives us eyes to see Jesus, ourselves, and each other from His perspective, and that enables us to think and act more like Christ. This enables us to love our neighbors and love ourselves because we are confident in who we are in Him and realize we are nothing apart from Him (John 15:5). The life of Christ can be fully present through us in word and in deed. Faith in His absolute authority is all that is required, and as our faith increases, our ability to hear God's voice and our courage and desire to follow Him will also grow.

When He talks of their losing their selves, He means only abandoning the clamor of self-will; once they have done that, He really gives them back all their personality, and boasts (I am afraid, sincerely) that when they are wholly His they will be more themselves than ever."[5] — C.S. Lewis, *The Screwtape Letters*

Several years ago I read a popular book, *The Shack*, by William Paul Young. It contains a fictional conversation between the Holy Spirit and a man named Mack about a poisonous plant the Holy Spirit asked Mack to touch. Though it is fictitious, it contains a profound truth.

Mack asked, "If you had not told me this was safe to touch, would it have poisoned me?" The Holy Spirit replied, "Of course! But if I direct you to touch, that is different. For any created being, autonomy is lunacy. Freedom involves trust and obedience inside a relationship of love. So, if you are not hearing my voice, it would be wise to take the time to understand the nature of the plant."[6]

Unlike a plant, we have the ability to resist God's pruning on our lives, and we do. We have the ability to pull away, to even pull out our roots and plant them somewhere else. Though the entire countryside is His and He is never unaware or not in control of His fields, our choices to resist His directions and/or pruning do make a difference in whether we grow a little, or a lot, or remain a dormant seed. Our choices can even result in our death (Romans 8:6), and all of it affects the look and health of the entire garden.

Because of this, I have struggled most with how I am to make decisions and on what basis I am to decide what to do and what not to do. I see how people live. I understand the Church. I understand religion, and I understand State and the secular side of the culture. I see what is acceptable and what brings criticism on both sides of the coin, and I have come to understand that it is most definitely a two-sided coin, but I have also come to understand that, for the one who trusts in the Holy, Living God, it is still *one coin*, and His life through Christ embodies it all.

As Americans, there are many choices available to us. This freedom to choose does not, however, excuse the moral and spiritual responsibilities we as Christian believers must uphold that give reference to our choices.

Throughout Jesus' ministry, He allowed God to have His way with His life. Rather than control His own destiny, He submitted to the perfect will of God the Father. There was no interference from Jesus and because of that, God's will and purpose was free to unfold and evolve. His public ministry took roughly three years to complete. I can't help but wonder what the effects would be in our nation and world if we did the same — if we allowed God the Father, to transform us into the likeness of God the Son (which is His desire and purpose for our lives) without resistance?

We are a diverse nation where the majority claims to be Christian (nearly two out of every three adults).[7] Yet, reliable statistics and surveys (many conducted by the George Barna Group) indicate we all want a better world but very few are willing to do what it takes to make the world better. We want excellence without sacrifice; beauty without effort; quality without price; and gratification without the wait. If our needs are not met or our individual preferences not validated, more and more the government steps in to intervene, and all is resulting in a divided nation that boasts of "equal opportunity for all" while it erodes in self-righteousness, moral character, personal comforts, and paralyzing apathy.

An Impossible Situation?

In the seventeenth chapter of the book of John, Jesus' desire for believers to be unified is evident. He prayed that *"they will all be one, just as you and I are one,"* and we can be sure that God will answer this prayer because it is His will expressed directly from the mouth of His Son (John 17:21). However, if we define the Body of Christ by the visible Church, it appears as if the LORD's desire is impossible.

The world is hurting and lost. Every day, there are millions who scan the horizon for a glimmer of hope and wonder what is wrong with them and what it would be like for someone to believe in them. Every day, a child's spirit is crushed. Every day, a parent's dreams are destroyed. Every day, tragedy strikes, lives are wounded and souls are lost. The majority of the world's population doesn't even have what they need to meet basic needs. People everywhere are trying to make a difference but have separated themselves so that no one is achieving full capacity for effectual change, and I am afraid that we who belong to the Body of Christ have allowed this to happen to us as well.

The Body of Christ is meant to be an organism; something that when healthy, grows naturally. Instead, the Church has become an institution. It has become something that is fixed in its ways, managed by pride, and controlled by man (or the majority vote). I don't think that's what most of us want it to be, but I am sad to say that I believe that's what it has become.

As a result, we, as a body of believers, are gravely limited in our ability to impact the culture, and we don't even seem to be aware of it.

Organization is good and helps us communicate, unite and move forward effectively, but we have to make sure we stay focused on the right things.

As humans, we are naturally attracted to those who are like us and who share our opinions and preferences. There is nothing wrong with this, but if we are not careful, we can lose sight of what is truly important. Size and preferences, biblical interpretations, and programs and policies affect the organization of a congregation and the way in which they express themselves, but they do not promote or define health. The presence of Christ in the people of a local church body is the *only thing* that constitutes health. Being a Christian is not about going to church; it's about *being* the Church.

Jesus said that *"Any kingdom divided by civil war is doomed"*(Matthew 12: 25). He also said a few verses later that *"Anyone who isn't with me opposes me, and anyone who isn't working with me is actually working against me"* (Matthew 12:30).

Despite our differences, God loves and uses all of us who are rooted in Him. If we cannot all come to the table with understanding and love, mercy, and faith in a God who is bigger than our differences, then we are missing the opportunity for true fellowship and worship that pleases the Lord and moves His heart (James 3:17-18).

As individuals, if we are resisting God's direction through His Holy Spirit, then we are not working with Him and are actually working against Him. As the Body of Christ, if we are not listening to each other or working together because of differences in things outside of Christ, then we are impotent and the nation we inhabit is doomed. We cannot function properly or grow to our potential without each other, and yet we continue to try and we even justify it. It's heart-breaking, and it has cost us.

The reason the people of God are called to go out in the power of the Holy Spirit is because the power of God changes things in ways that cannot be altered or explained. If this was applied to the American Church and Christ truly lived through His people so that the Church was what it is supposed to be, then it seems right to assume that, with the majority of the U.S. claiming to be Christian, all other facets of American systems would be what they are supposed to be as well (or at least much closer). The best defense is a good offense, but one only has to look around to see that something is wrong.

The message of Christ never changes, but the Body of Christ must continue to breathe and grow *and mature* according to the wisdom of God. It takes all of our personalities, all of our thought processes, all of our passions, all of our experiences, and all of our gifts and talents and skills to make up the entire being of Christ. Even with that, there is still so much to Him that we do not understand. He is Truth, but the ways in which He expresses Himself are beyond what any one person, one local church, one denomination, or one way of ministry can accomplish. We need each other to complete each other and even then we fall short of all that is Christ.

Nothing is more attractive than Jesus, but if we are not acting and communicating with His character both within the Body of Christ and outside of it, then the only way we are going to grow is through dynamic pastors and worldly imitations because we're no different than anyone else. We have confused being contemporary with relevance and define our success by the number of people we attract to our services rather than by the reflection of Christ in our lives and His impact in our communities. A sense of control and lack of diversity makes things easier, but they also allow pride to run dangerously rampant, and when this occurs under the direction of ambitious leaders who conduct themselves like CEOs rather than humble servants, the result can look a lot like my life did when I was comfortable underneath the layers of illusion. It looks good. It feels good, but it's not what God designed and, therefore, limits His power and effectiveness in our own lives as well as in the lives of others.

Olivia asked me at a very young age if God shared His glory, and the answer is an emphatic "No!" As long as we are living according to the Spirit and allowing the presence of Christ to touch those before us, our attention is focused on the right things, and the Body of Christ is free to evolve naturally according to the creative and infinite mind of Christ — not the limited mind of man — and, thus, remain both fluid and effective within our changing cultures. The Church will grow and have relevant impact when we individually understand our poverty, when we see through His eyes, and when He is our expectation.

What the law allows or prohibits, whether or not the Ten Commandments are posted, or whether or not the president prays are all important things, but they are actually just the expressions of what lies internally. When Christ truly lives through His Church, *when His life lives through His people*, the externals reflect more and more of His character. But, even if they do not, He is *still* in control, and our focus should not deflect to change the externals outside of our desire for Christ or we will sink our nation as we walk the road of good intentions and righteous indignations (Matthew 14:29-30).

> About the general connection between Christianity and politics, our position is more delicate. Certainly we do not want men to allow their Christianity to flow over into their political life, for the establishment of anything like a really just society would be a major disaster. On the other hand we do want, and want very much, to make men treat Christianity as a means; preferably, of course, as a means to their own advancement, but, failing that, as a means to anything — even to social justice.[8] — C.S. Lewis, *The Screwtape Letters*

There is nothing we can do for God other than walk in the freedom He has given us and surrender to Him our lives as vessels through which He then uses to touch others wherever we are. If we really want to make a difference, we must be willing to hold lightly to all that we have (understanding it's not ours any way), all that we desire (knowing God's ways are best), and all that we are (realizing He created us uniquely for a purpose that can only be found in Him), and allow Him to lead us.

We must let Him live through us and speak for Himself by stepping out of the comfortable walls of the church and going beyond ourselves to extend a helping hand in everyday life. We must do what we can to lift and empower our neighbors in times of need. We must value the lives of others and implore accountability for a stabilized foundation on which we all can grow. We must listen more, speak less, and do what we can to maintain the moral strength of our nation by letting the Church be the Church, letting government be government, understanding the difference and where we all fit. It appears risky, but it's not. It's just hard to do because it goes against our controlling nature.

If we do not seek the Kingdom of God first and above all else, then our reasoning, our abilities, our desires, our fears, our comforts, our prejudices, our pride, and every other thing we value more than God Himself will interfere with His intentions (Matthew 6:31-33). Things happen for a reason, but it's not always God's reason. More often than not, things happen because of our own sin and selfishness and even our own ignorance and good intentions. God is the One who is left with the chaos and is working it together for the good of those who love Him and are called according to His purpose (Romans 8:28), but it takes time. It is His will that not one should perish

(Matthew 18:14), and the sooner we cooperate, the sooner He can have His way, for when we are united by Christ, we are one in Christ (Galatians 3:26-28). Unity always paves the way for success.

> Make them holy by your truth; teach them your word, which is truth. Just as you sent me into the world, I am sending them into the world. And I give myself as a holy sacrifice for them so they can be made holy by your truth. I am praying not only for these disciples but also for all who will ever believe in me through their message. I pray that they will all be one, just as you and I are one — as you are in me, Father, and I am in you. And may they be in us so that the world will believe you sent me. (John 17:17-21 62)

Though we do not respond to Jesus in the same way, we can be sure that His response to each of us is consistent and grounded in the essence of who He is. Jesus changed the world by being Himself, and His desire is to continue to change the world by being Himself uniquely through each of us. Perhaps the greatest command to love God with all that we are and the next greatest command to love one another as we also love ourselves are the only unifying forces available to us, and *perhaps*, like Eve, we do not understand the magnitude of our choices.

Her personal choice and influence ushered in a Savior. Ours just might bring Him back (2 Peter 3:11-12).

Bedtime Stories

I have certain bedtime "rituals" with each of my children that takes about 45 — 60 minutes to put everyone to bed. That seems like a long time, but really it's only 20 minutes per child and some days these are the only one-on-one times I have with them. There are nights — many nights — when I just don't think I have an hour to say goodnight. My children aren't babies and they could handle it, of course, but an hour of tucking them in is a gift of time. I understand that now more than ever.

The boys share a room, and since John likes his back scratched in *complete* silence with the light *off*, the rituals usually start with my youngest son, Sam. Reading is our thing. We've been on the Dr. Seuss books for a while — several of which I used to read with my young clients when I was practicing as a speech-language pathologist.

One night, Sam noticed on the inside of the book cover that I had written my name and the word "speech." Remember, *nothing* goes unnoticed by him, so I had to explain why the word "speech" was written in the book and said something like, "I used to be a speech pathologist just like Ms. Allyn (Sam's current therapist) and used this book to help the children I saw, like she helps you." I answered several questions about all of that, and then Sam asked a question that completely stumped me, "Well, what are you now?"

I figured a good and accurate response would be, "I am your mom," but he already knew that, and unfortunately for me I knew it wouldn't satisfy him. He was looking for a different answer, and I really had no idea what to say.

Lying in bed with my youngest son who was born on the other side of the world to a birth mother and father he will never know this side of heaven and is now my precious possession, things have changed. I have come to more crossroads than I ever thought was even possible, and in each stage of the journey, the opportunity to surrender more of my life and place it under the authority of God through Christ has arisen.

If Sam had asked me the same question at a different time in my life, depending on when it was, I could have answered confidently, a number of different things. That night, however, in fact, still today, I don't have a person (actually I have many, I just see them from the right perspective now), a profession, a title, a home, my health, or even a bank account to default to.

My answer to Sam's question is this: I am a servant and a child of the Most High God. Wherever He places me and in whatever capacity He places me in — whether it is in the local church or in the community, whether in this country or in another, as a leader or a follower, an entrepreneur or advisor, a teacher, a writer, a wife, a mother, a daughter, a sister, a neighbor, or a friend, my goal is to serve Him by serving others and using all He has given me to make a difference that not only meets needs and improves the quality of life for others but unveils who He is. He is the One I belong to. It is His voice I want to hear above all others. It is He to whom I long to be true.

> You didn't choose me. I chose you. I appointed you to go and produce lasting fruit, so that the Father will give you whatever you ask for, using my name. This is my command: Love each other. (John 15:16-17)

Notes

[1] Oswald Chambers, *My Utmost for His Highest* (Oswald Chambers Publication Association, Ltd. 1992), March 12.

[2] Ibid, May 6.

[3] Hannah Hurnard, *Hinds' Feet on High Places* (Uhrichsville: Barbour Publishing, Inc.), 15, 214.

[4] Gregory Boyd, *The Myth of a Christian Nation* (Grand Rapids: Zondervan, 2005), 132.

[5] C. S. Lewis, *The Screwtape Letters* (New York: Harper Collins, 1996), 65.

[6] William Paul Young, *The Shack* (Newbury Park, Windblown Media, 2007), 132-133.

[7] George Barna, *The Seven Faith Tribes* (Carol Stream: Tyndale House Publishers, 2009), 16-17.

[8] Lewis, *The Screwtape Letters*, 126.

The Bridge Builder

An old man going a lone highway
Came at the evening, cold and gray,
To a chasm vast and wide and steep,
With waters rolling cold and deep.
The old man crossed in the twilight dim,
The sullen stream had no fears for him;
But he turned when safe on the other side,
And built a bridge to span the tide.

"Old man," said a fellow pilgrim near,
"You are wasting your strength with building here.
Your journey will end with the ending day,
You never again will pass this way.
You've crossed the chasm, deep and wide,
Why build you this bridge at eventide?"

The builder lifted his old gray head.
"Good friend, in the path I have come," he said
"There followeth after me today
A youth whose feet must pass this way.
The chasm that was as nought to me
To that fair-haired youth may a pitfall be;
He, too, must cross in the twilight dim —
Good friend, I am building this bridge for him."

— WILL ALLEN DROMGOOLE

Dromgoogle, Will Allen, "The Bridge Builder," as cited at <www.poetryfoundation.org/poem/237102> from *Father: An Anthology of Verse* (EP Dutton & Company, 1931) 86.

CHAPTER SEVEN
Proving Wisdom

Dedicated to the children of South Arkansas.
In honor of Justin, Jordan, Hunter, Heath, Kaitlyn, Curt, Sami, Luke and Kaelon

...wisdom is shown to be right by its results.
— Matthew 11:19

When I first began organizing my thoughts and memories in writing, my purpose was to put into place the things I most wanted to share with my children just in case I didn't get the chance to do it personally. There was so much I needed to tell them and to teach them, but at their young ages they weren't ready to receive all that I wanted to give.

The desire to leave them with a lasting legacy remains my primary motivation for writing, but it has grown into something more.

I learned a valuable lesson several years ago while watching one of Oprah Winfrey's shows. I don't remember why I was home that day from work, but I do remember sitting in the den of our brand new home and being stunned by what I was watching.

It was a segment about a repulsive situation going on in another country where young girls were being attacked and having the very special and private parts of their bodies violently mutilated because of some sick belief. It was truly awful, and though it was over ten years ago, I am still moved by it as I write this today.

Just as I was wishing I hadn't seen that show, the words of Oprah echoed, "Now that you know, you are responsible." And, she was right. If I have knowledge of something that is true and affects the lives of others then I am responsible for what I do with that knowledge.

Our hearts deceive us. People, things, ideas, and situations that we think will be there forever only last for a short period. They fade with time and are false securities. Only the Word of the LORD stands forever (Isaiah 40:8, 1 John 2:15-17).

In a way, we are all taking part in a great performance. No matter who we are, our lives are made to shine like "stars in the universe," (Philippians 2:15) but it is the Person of Jesus Christ that solidifies our performance and enables us to shine with a lasting impression (John 1:1-5). His unending, unfailing love changes us from shooting stars that fade to enduring stars that last forever, and it is our mission to bring others to the stage by revealing to all earth and heaven that the music of life is not in conditions or things or anything this world has to offer, but the music of life is in our own souls.

> Paganini, the great violinist, came out before his audience one day and made the discovery just as they ended their applause that there was something wrong with his violin. He looked at it a second and then saw that it was not his famous and valuable one.
>
> He felt paralyzed for a moment, then turned to his audience and told them there had been some mistake and he did not have his own violin. He stepped back behind the curtain thinking that it was still where he had left it, but discovered that someone had stolen his and left that old secondhand one in its place. He remained back of the curtain a moment, then came out before his audience and said: 'Ladies and Gentlemen: I will show you that the music is not in the instrument, but in the soul.' And he played as he had never played before; and out of that secondhand instrument, the music poured forth until the audience was enraptured with enthusiasm and the applause almost lifted the ceiling of the building, because the man had revealed to them that music was not in the machine but in his own soul.[1]

It is Christ's song, played through the lives of His people that speaks and overflows in a melody only the heart can hear and respond to. He changes things. He changes us, no matter who we are. And, that performance reveals a reality that brings people to their feet and heals their hearts and binds their wounds with a hope that will never fade.

If only every person could understand this at a young age. What a difference it would make for them personally as they grew and for all they influenced!

Though we are all born with a sinful nature, our young lives are not yet tarnished by counterfeit truths, so we have the ability to perceive what is real and true without interference. Children are disturbed by the tiniest morsel of evil and thrilled by the goodness of love. They are a gift, and loving them and caring for them is a responsibility and a privilege — whether they are born to us or not.

My children stir something in me that is inexpressible. I don't deserve them and am often times overwhelmed by the graciousness of God in giving them to me. They are tremendous and priceless gifts yet a heavy responsibility. If Phil and I are not deliberate in our teaching and care of them, we are careless with our riches, and, frankly, careless with the riches of the world.

We don't get a second chance. Every moment passed is a moment gone. They are exhausting and challenging. They are full of adventure and excitement. They are sweet and sometimes not so sweet, innocent and mischievous. They push every limit we set and for sure, every button I have, but I am a better person because of them. They have changed my life, and God has taught me more through them than I could have learned without them.

> *Children are God's apostles, day by day, sent forth to preach of love, hope, and peace. — James Russell Lowell*

I was walking through my house after everyone had gone to bed when my eyes fell on a picture of Olivia taken when she was about 18-months old. In the picture, she was wearing a simple, white cotton dress with an angel embroidered in pastel colors in the center of her chest. Over the angel were the words, "I believe." Her piercing but tranquil blue eyes seemed to make the statement without the words. She was beautiful, and still is. As I gazed at that picture, my eyes filled with tears and somewhere deep in my soul I sighed in agreement.

I believe there is a greater good, and, though that may mean different things to different people, it doesn't change reality; that the plight for humanity and preservation of the earth are witnesses to this goodness in the hearts of man and stems from the heart of Almighty God who cares for His creation.

I believe mankind was created within a framework of natural and divine law that, when lived within, does not define our worth, but protects our well-being.

I believe human life is made in the image of God and is, therefore, worthy and precious regardless of what it looks like or how comfortable it makes us feel; that good is greater than evil, and doing what is right in the eyes of God will always work for our best and prevail victorious in the end.

I believe every life is called by God through Jesus Christ but only those who respond are chosen; that freedom is a gift, but one which holds us accountable for our choices.

I believe only love enables us to dignify one another without compromise of character or succumbing to judgment; that it penetrates boundaries of differences among us out of the motivation it causes to act beyond ourselves.

I believe we should help those in need because they need it and not because we think it will change the world, though it will; that life is meant to be lived, not endured, that we are all flawed and imperfect, needing the forgiveness and mercy of others to help us embrace who we are and who we are not.

I believe intelligence and wisdom are two different things; that the beginning of wisdom is the fear of God, and that a small child can both lead and teach us.

I believe wisdom sees clearly what reason cannot and that authentic leadership recognizes its Authority, never forgetting its accountability to those who follow.

The Heart of the Battle

Like flowers depend on water and nutrients within the soil it is planted, children depend on us. They are strong and resilient yet fragile and vulnerable. Each one is like a seed, that when properly nurtured, has the potential for full growth. They are pliable. They are precious, *and they are in danger.*

Research shows that all facets of moral and spiritual development begin as early as age two, and a basic understanding of what is right and wrong is established by age five.[2] By age nine, moral and spiritual foundations are in place, and by the age of 13, the beliefs and foundations on which all thoughts are processed and decisions are made are determined by a worldview that changes very little unless something significant transpires to shift or alter the way that person thinks.[3]

Since the beginning of time, facts and myths have intertwined and weaved suspicious conspiracies, cults, religions, and gods. Depending on who we are, the beliefs of the culture we are born into generally become our beliefs by default, and those moral and spiritual beliefs (and the degrees by which we are convicted by them) affect every decision we make.

It is easy to entertain almost any belief until it is weighed by another. The perception may be a reality in one person's mind, but looking at the issue objectively, his or her understanding may or may not be accurate. If what a person understands to be true is actually NOT true then his or her perception (or reality) is actually an *illusion*, a false perception or reality. And, that false perception will lead him or her to draw false conclusions, share false information, and make choices that are based on something that either does not exist or will not last. In essence, that person is believing, living, and sharing a lie, and lies steal the blessings God has in store for us and replaces them with counterfeits that take us down paths that lead away from the one bridge (the Person of Jesus Christ) that takes us home and gives us life (2 Corinthians 11:3-5).

We live in a world where many, maybe even the majority, believe what they hear without questioning. We believe what we read without researching. We believe what we see without looking a little deeper. The information gets in our minds and becomes a part of our thinking, and then we believe that because we think it, it must be right, and everyone else needs to listen to what we have to say. We may have facts and we definitely have opinions but we are unable to tell the difference between them and seldom take time to discern how they might work within the context of a larger world view that exists outside of our own little corner of it.

We are so desensitized by the amount and frequency of biased, corrupted information and imagery that comes at us from all directions that we are not diligently guarding and protecting our most valuable possession — the free will to control our thoughts.

As children develop perspectives and patterns of thinking that dictate their decision-making, it is one of our most important responsibilities as parents and ambassadors for Christ to strategically and deliberately guide them through this process. Doing so without concern for the moral and spiritual development of our children would be to neglect the foundation on which their lives have been created and in which all decisions are ultimately made.[4]

The greatest potential we have for impact lies in the hearts and minds of our children and youth. They are the battlefront, and we bear the primary responsibility for how this battle turns out.[5] How tragic it is to neglect these precious seedlings just under our feet because we don't realize our responsibilities and power to make both temporal and eternal impact in their young lives! Knowledge is one thing. Wisdom is quite another (Proverbs 1:7, Proverbs 8:10-36, James 3: 13-18).

Phil and I want our children to be where we are forever, but more than that, we want them to be with their LORD and God. Although they are the ones who must receive and then choose for themselves what they do with what they know, there is nothing we could give them in this life that is more important than God Himself (Colossians 2:2). He is Truth, and our need for Him is the only way we can truly know Him — the only gift with lasting treasures (Matthew 6:19-21, Matthew 7: 9-11).

Our lives are the examples that must point to Him in all that we do — trusting God beyond our common sense and allowing everyday life to be teachable moments. It's not a manmade plan but is, rather, a plan that is written into the souls of humanity by God Himself (Psalm 19:7-11; Proverbs 1-4; Proverbs 6:20-23).

As parents, we are responsible for preparing our children to not only stand strong in this culture but to engage and make impact. If we are Christians, then the standard for us is God through Christ — a standard that does not change depending on what we think. He is absolute truth. His authority, His ways, and His character do not change based on our preferences, comforts, emotions or ideas, and if He is not our first priority, then no matter how good or well intentioned we are, we will misguide our children more than we may realize.

As the Body of Christ, we are responsible for living our lives exactly as the Lord God instructs us to live — without apology but with love, humility and mercy (1 John 2:27; Micah 6:8). Again, the standard for us is God through Christ — *a standard that does not change depending on our preferences, comforts, emotions or ideas.* He is life and all that it entails, and His presence changes the course of our lives and those who we love and influence.

> Work for the peace and prosperity of the city where I sent you…Pray to the LORD for it, for its welfare will determine your welfare. (Jeremiah 29:7)

In my second year of graduate school at Memphis State (now Memphis University), I did a clinical rotation at St. Jude Children's Hospital under the direction of my professor, Dr. Joel Kahane. The first time we walked into the front doors of that hospital, the sight of so many sick children and their families made my heart sink.

I was 23 at the time and had never seen the effects of disease as I did in the waiting room that first day. My excitement over the rotation quickly faded to sadness, and I told my professor on the way back from the hospital that I didn't want to go back.

He said, "Jennifer, if you don't go back, that is your choice to make, but those children will be there whether you are there or not. Their situations will not change just because you choose not to be a part of it. However, those who do choose to face it have at least the opportunity to help make a difference in their lives." I have never forgotten those words.

Our actions influence others and are a power we underestimate and responsibility we neglect every day. People need Hope, not a best effort or watered-down sentiment.

Satan waits to twist truth and create false evidence that supports the deception in our minds. Those of us who share faith in Jesus Christ have a great responsibility not only to each other but to this generation of children and adults by exposing this darkness in the light of what is true.

Despite the richness of family and providence that many of us share and, sadly, many of us do not, we all are born to live as children under the heritage of a Living God (Romans 8:15-17, 23, Galatians 4:4-7, Ephesians 1: 5-14). The Holy, Living, God Almighty is waiting to adopt each one of us through the life of His Son (a very part of God Himself). Yet, because of sin and the prideful nature we are born with, we make choices that serve our cravings. Each of us is born with a nature that is contrary to God's nature (Romans 8:17), but we are also born in His image (Genesis 1:26-27). Because of that, we each have a deep desire to belong, a desire to live with purpose and to love and be loved. It is something built within all of us regardless of our differences and reflects our Creator whether we recognize it or not.

My dear friend, Pastor Lane Harrison, said it best in a recent email, "When a church is about everything, it inevitably becomes about nothing." Missions entails the entire life of Christ to the one who is standing in front of us no matter where we are, and if that one is a child, you better believe the stakes are high (Matthew 18:1-6, 10-11, 14).

In order to be responsible with what we know, it will require courage and determination, open communication, healthy partnerships, and true fellowship — things only the character of Christ can achieve through His Body positioned throughout our nation and world.

There is a power in the Person of Jesus that heals all who are touched by Him, but we cannot expect people who do not know Christ to act and think according to His nature and values, and we cannot blame them for not understanding when we ourselves don't live what we say we believe. Before we can change the world or the culture around us, we have to first change ourselves. We have to dig in where we are, and we have to keep going back.

Embracing Our Heritage

Our society is deteriorating because we are allowing the lives of our children to deteriorate. Thousands and thousands of children in the U.S. and millions worldwide do not have the love, the support, the knowledge, or the opportunities they need to reach their potential or know their worth, and they grow to become parents of children who repeat the same patterns.

Shaping the way a young person thinks and cultivating his or her character with the presence of Christ in us would not only redefine the future for that child, it would redefine the culture of the next generation by helping to break destructive cycles that keep them from living full and abundant lives.

My cousin, Phoebe Sue, has masterfully compiled historical information on the ancestry of her parents over many generations. Because her mother and my grandfather were brother and sister, my family has benefitted from the knowledge as well. Through her (and through the process of adopting Sam), I have learned about the importance of our life stories.

Research has shown that children who know about their familial roots possess a strong "intergenerational self" which is the sense of belonging to something larger than themselves. As a result, they demonstrate more self-confidence and resilience to stress than those who do not have this knowledge or understanding.[6]

This was evidenced in our son, Sam, when his fears were calmed simply by showing him the picture album with his foster family (all that he knew) included with his adoptive family when we were still in China waiting to bring him home for the first time. It was a nonverbal way of saying, "This is where you came from and this is where you are going. This is who you are and who you belong to, and it's not going to change no matter what happens."

But, our heritage is so much more than our earthly lineage. We are spiritual beings born from a spiritual Father who is God and Savior and

Guide. To successfully navigate the journey of life, children must possess a worldview that is based on Him. Otherwise, their perceptions of reality will be an illusion and their journey in life will be marred with the pain of either figuring that out or believing the lies that steal true hope.

To effectively stand in the gap, we have to shift the way we think. We have to do something different if we want better results, and I am certain it will require a collaborative effort. The power of unity blazes trails we don't realize are there, but *only the Church (the living, breathing Body of Christ) can find them.*

> So, when you see the Levitical priests carrying the Ark of the Covenant of the LORD your God, move out from your positions and follow them. Since you have never traveled this way before, they will guide you." (Joshua 3:3-4)

> …For you are a chosen people. You are royal priests, a holy nation, God's very own possession. As a result, you can show others the goodness of God. (1 Peter 2:9)

I am amazed by people like my husband. He's not perfect (as none of us are), but Phil's humility and confidence in who he is in God and who God is in Him enables him as a man to hold me loosely and to not take himself so seriously. He lets others off the hook (including me), letting them be who they are while at the same time being true to who he is. He understands that only God through His Holy Spirit can teach without wounding because he himself has hurt others and has also been the one wounded. His abandonment to the teaching of God through His Holy Spirit and the spiritual maturity that has resulted has come at a price and has been a great example for me. Christ's presence in Phil has taught me and led me, many times without him even knowing it or saying a word.

The world is full of self-appointed, man-elected leaders, but true leaders are ordained by God and marked by His Spirit, like Phil. Together, we make up the Body of Christ, and His mind and heart, His feet and hands, His voice and character, His strength and creativity are positioned all over this nation and world in each of us just waiting for us to awaken to who He is and what that means for us (Ephesians 1:19-23).

Jesus is God's will and when He lives through us, we too are His will. If we work in and through our positions in daily life using the unique sets of skills and talents, gifts and resources God has given to each of us to influence those around us, we can make a difference in this generation (and in the child in all of us) that will bring honor and praise to our Lord and God (2 Corinthians 9:6-15, 2 Corinthians 10:13). We can build a solid foundation for the Kingdom on earth to grow as it is in heaven just like our brothers and sisters built the wall in Nehemiah's day — with different people, in different places, and in different ways but all at the same time.

> It's not important who does the planting, or who does the watering. What's important is that God makes the seed grow. The one who plants and the one who waters work together with the same purpose. And both will be rewarded for their own hard work. For we are both God's workers. And you are God's field. You are God's building...But whoever is building on this foundation must be very careful. For no one can lay any foundation other than the one we already have — Jesus Christ. Anyone who builds on that foundation may use a variety of materials — gold, silver, jewels, wood, hay, or straw. But on the judgment day, fire will reveal what kind of work each builder has done. The fire will show if a person's work has any value. If the work survives, that builder will receive a reward. But if the work is burned up, the builder will suffer great loss. (1 Corinthians 3:7-15)

> Don't you realize that all of you together are the temple of God and that the Spirit of God lives in you? ...For God's temple is holy, and you are that temple. Stop deceiving yourselves. If you think you are wise by this world's standards you need to become a fool to be truly wise. For the wisdom of this world is foolishness to God. So don't boast about following a particular human leader. For everything belongs to you...and you belong to Christ, and Christ belongs to God. (1 Corinthians 3:16-19, 21-23)

Living Our Destiny

I was tucking Olivia in bed one night when she reached up and took my face in her hands and said in disbelief, "Momma, you're getting wrinkles on your face!" Then, after careful exploration of my face, her eyes swelled with tears and she said, "I don't want you to get older."

It took me a minute to get over the shock about the wrinkles, but the innocence and depth of that moment surprised me even more. What nine-year-old notices her mother's wrinkles, and, for that matter, cares about it? It was a moment I have pondered time and time again.

Olivia's comments were true, and so was her sadness. She knows that my getting older means my life is getting shorter. Every day brings us closer to our last day, for there is a time for all of us on earth when we must depart from our loved ones and the life we know. That day will come for me and for those I love, and it will be sad. Reality will not be altered, and our fears will not lessen the pace of its coming but only steal the time of the present. It comes every moment we breathe. It comes every night when the sun sets. And, it comes with the dawn of a new morning.

I'm not sure what Job did with his life once God restored him, but I have a pretty good idea what I am going to do with mine.

May I live what I know each day I am given and do it in a way that loves and leads well on behalf of God's children and the world for which Christ died. Because, you see, like the words on Olivia's dress, ***I Believe… and it's not over.***

> But forget all that — it is nothing compared to what I am going to do. For I am about to do something new. See, I have already begun! Do you not see it? I will make a pathway through the wilderness…so my chosen people can be refreshed. I have made Israel for myself, and they will someday honor me before the whole world. (Isaiah 43:18-21)

Notes

[1] L.B. Cowman, *Streams in the Desert* (The Zondervan Corporation, 1996), 288-289.

[2] George Barna, *Transforming Children Into Spiritual Champions* (Ventura: Regal Books by Gospel Light, 2003), 47.

[3] Ibid, 34, 37, 47, 58.

[4] Ibid, 30-32.

[5] Ibid., 57.

[6] Bruce Feiler, *This Life*, "The Stories That Bind Us," March 15, 2013, (www.nytimes.com).

Closing Prayer

Dedicated to the child in all of us.

I pray that your love will overflow more and more,
> and that you will keep on growing in knowledge and understanding.

For I want you to understand what really matters
> so that you may live pure and blameless lives until the day of Christ's return.

May you always be filled with the fruit of your salvation —
> the righteous character produced in your life by Jesus Christ — for this will bring much glory and praise to God.

— Philippians 1:9-11

Suggested Reading

George Barna, *Transforming Children Into Spiritual Champions*
Henry Blackaby and Carrie Blackaby Webb, *Prepared to be God's Vessel*
E.M. Bounds, *The Necessity of Prayer*
Gregory A. Boyd, *The Myth of a Christian Nation*
Oswald Chambers, *My Utmost for His Highest*
Don Colbert, *The Seven Pillars of Health*
L.B. Cowman, *Streams in the Desert*
Jim Cymbala, *Fresh Wind, Fresh Fire*
Richard J. Foster, *Celebration of Discipline*
Napoleon Hill, *Think and Grow Rich*
Hannah Hurnard, *Hinds' Feet On High Places*
Timothy Keller, *The Reason for God*
C.S. Lewis, *Mere Christianity*
C.S. Lewis, *The Screwtape Letters*
Josh McDowell, *The Last Christian Generation*
Beth Moore, *Jesus, the One and Only*
Stormie Omartian, *The Power of a Praying Parent*
John Ortberg, *The Life You've Always Wanted*
Dr. M. Scott Peck, *The Road Less Traveled*
Kerry and Chris Shook, *One Month to Live: 30 Days to a No Regrets Life*
Richard Stearns, *The Hole in Our Gospel*
Mother Teresa, *A Simple Path*
A.W. Tozer, *The Pursuit of God*
Rick Warren, *The Purpose Driven Life*
Philip Yancey, *Church, Why Bother?*
William Paul Young, *The Shack*
Sarah Young, *Jesus Calling*

www.ingramcontent.com/pod-product-compliance
Lightning Source LLC
Chambersburg PA
CBHW071227160426
43196CB00012B/2430